CAMBRIDGE LIBRARY COLLECTION

Books of enduring scholarly value

Women's Writing

The later twentieth century saw a huge wave of academic interest in women's writing, which led to the rediscovery of neglected works from a wide range of genres, periods and languages. Many books that were immensely popular and influential in their own day are now studied again, both for their own sake and for what they reveal about the social, political and cultural conditions of their time. A pioneering resource in this area is Orlando: Women's Writing in the British Isles from the Beginnings to the Present (http://orlando.cambridge.org), which provides entries on authors' lives and writing careers, contextual material, timelines, sets of internal links, and bibliographies. Its editors have made a major contribution to the selection of the works reissued in this series within the Cambridge Library Collection, which focuses on non-fiction publications by women on a wide range of subjects from astronomy to biography, music to political economy, and education to prison reform.

Women and Work

Emily Pfeiffer (1827–90) was a British poet, writer and feminist. Best known for her poetry and sonnets, Pfeiffer also published essays and articles for numerous publications addressing the status of women in contemporary society. This volume, first published in 1888, contains Pfeiffer's analysis of social attitudes towards higher education and professional work for women. She explores in detail the social attitudes which discouraged women from attempting higher education, and describes and refutes contemporary medical opinions concerning the supposed dangers to health women faced in pursuit of it. She also presents an economic argument advocating the entry of women both to higher education and to professional employment. This volume provides a valuable analysis of contemporary attitudes to women's education during a period when the beginnings of change were accompanied by much controversy. For more information on this author, see http://orlando.cambridge.org/public/svPeople?person_id=pfeiem

T0382299

Cambridge University Press has long been a pioneer in the reissuing of out-of-print titles from its own backlist, producing digital reprints of books that are still sought after by scholars and students but could not be reprinted economically using traditional technology. The Cambridge Library Collection extends this activity to a wider range of books which are still of importance to researchers and professionals, either for the source material they contain, or as landmarks in the history of their academic discipline.

Drawing from the world-renowned collections in the Cambridge University Library, and guided by the advice of experts in each subject area, Cambridge University Press is using state-of-the-art scanning machines in its own Printing House to capture the content of each book selected for inclusion. The files are processed to give a consistently clear, crisp image, and the books finished to the high quality standard for which the Press is recognised around the world. The latest print-on-demand technology ensures that the books will remain available indefinitely, and that orders for single or multiple copies can quickly be supplied.

The Cambridge Library Collection will bring back to life books of enduring scholarly value (including out-of-copyright works originally issued by other publishers) across a wide range of disciplines in the humanities and social sciences and in science and technology.

Women and Work

*An Essay Treating on the Relation to
Health and Physical Development, of the
Higher Education of Girls, and the Intellectual
or More Systematised Effort of Women*

EMILY PFEIFFER

CAMBRIDGE UNIVERSITY PRESS

Cambridge, New York, Melbourne, Madrid, Cape Town, Singapore,
São Paolo, Delhi, Dubai, Tokyo, Mexico City

Published in the United States of America by Cambridge University Press, New York

www.cambridge.org
Information on this title: www.cambridge.org/9781108021760

© in this compilation Cambridge University Press 2010

This edition first published 1888
This digitally printed version 2010

ISBN 978-1-108-02176-0 Paperback

WOMEN AND WORK.

An Essay

TREATING ON

THE RELATION TO HEALTH AND PHYSICAL DEVELOPMENT,
OF THE HIGHER EDUCATION OF GIRLS,
AND THE INTELLECTUAL OR MORE SYSTEMATISED EFFORT
OF WOMEN.

BY

EMILY PFEIFFER,

AUTHOR OF "GERARD'S MONUMENT," "UNDER THE ASPENS,"
"THE RHYME OF THE LADY OF THE ROCK,"
"FLYING LEAVES FROM EAST TO WEST," "SONNETS,"
ETC. ETC. ETC.

LONDON:
TRÜBNER & CO., LUDGATE HILL.
1888.

Ballantyne Press
BALLANTYNE, HANSON AND CO.
EDINBURGH AND LONDON

CONTENTS.

———◆———

PART I.

THE SENTIMENTAL DIFFICULTY CONSIDERED.

A

I.

"Prendre le parti des femmes, est-ce vouloir redresser les erreurs des hommes ou leur mauvaise foi ?"—M. FELIX REMO.

MY object in the present essay is to present the problem of the enlarged sphere of action to which the women of our generation lay claim, under each of the three aspects from which it is commonly regarded, and to supply the best answers I have been able to arrive at, to the most forcible of the objections urged against it.

It may be said that this movement, which is looked on by thoughtful minds as one of the most important, if not actually the most important, of those which will set their mark upon our era, is at this time fairly on its way; that the more thorough education of girls of all classes is already widely diffused, and that new modes of activity for women are opening year by year. All this is true; but, when fully admitted, it still remains that some slight review, some further revindication of the subject as it at present manifests itself, may not be without its use; and chiefly because there are still abroad certain erroneous notions with reference to this question, which have not been adequately refuted, and

which, from their insidious nature, are well calculated
to retard its satisfactory solution.   Chief among these
may be reckoned the fears kept alive by the reiterated
cries of alarmists, as to the effect upon the health of
the individual and the race, of the higher education
to which the sex lays claim.   I should wish it to be
understood that what I have to offer in this connection is not intended solely for assailants, or for those
whose minds are not fully made up, but in at least
equal measure for those students who are undergoing
the process which is known under the above title.
Nothing could be better designed for procuring the
evil effects attributed to it than that morbid habit of
physical introspection which is being forced upon young
girls by the nervous terrors, real or assumed, of those
who are watching their doings from without.

I cannot do better than quote in this place the
sensible words of Mrs. Bryant, D.Sc., in a lecture
delivered at the College of Preceptors, November
1884 :—

"In the early days of the overwork panic, when
members of the medical profession first made against
the scholastic profession the charge of general over-
pressure, and the public mind became alarmed, and
worked itself into an attitude of terror at every passing
shadow of fatigue, like that of a nervous child who
fears familiar objects in the dark, the sanguine amongst
us hoped that this panic, like others, would rise to a
critical height, and then subside to the quiet level of a

reasonable caution which is neither fear nor rashness.
We were therefore content to defend ourselves merely
at special points where attacked, and were particularly
slow to bring forward the counter-charges against our
friends the doctors, which nevertheless have been in our
minds all along.   We have not been indifferent, for we
have suffered; but we have been very meek in deed, if
not in thought.   Besides, we were busy, and believed
that truth would triumph in the long-run if we did
our duty, whether we explained it or not.   It has not,
however, begun to triumph yet, and now I think it
will not triumph till we who are teachers, and
especially we who are teachers of girls and most
attacked, explain ourselves more plainly than we have
done hitherto.   This panic will not easily die down of
its own accord; just as a cholera panic aids in the
propagation of cholera, *so does an overwork panic aid*
in the production of that abnormal condition of body
and mind which it is the custom to attribute to over-
work.   I therefore think it worth while to make some
attempt at an explanation, in my own manner, of the
position taken, I believe, by the large majority of
teachers in the controversy on this subject.   We
believe that we see aspects of the question which the
doctor, as doctor merely, could hardly be expected to
imagine; and we found our opinions on a knowledge
of children who are well, no less than of children who
are ill; whereas the medical man knows only the latter."

Mrs. Bryant goes on, from the depth of her personal

experience, to classify girl-students, and to divide them
into the few who are over-zealous, the many who are
normally well-balanced, mind and body, the many more
who are indolent, and into three other categories which
it is not necessary here to particularise. The whole
of this lecture, which has since been printed and
issued in pamphlet form by the firm of Francis
Hodgson, 89 Farringdon Street, E.C., is worthy of
attentive perusal; and had its circulation been wider, I
might not have felt myself called upon to dwell at
such length as I propose to do upon this particular
aspect of my subject; although even had it met with
all the attention it deserves, the re-enforcement of its
propositions by the distinguished authorities I have
been able to bring together would, seeing the weight
of inertia, as well as of positive hostility which sur-
rounds this question, have been no more than what is
needed to make a sensible impression upon it.

But paramount in importance, at least for the present moment, as this view of my theme undoubtedly
is, it is far from standing alone; and any attempt to
resume the actual state of the case in regard to
women and their claims as against opponents of their
progress, would be wanting in true perspective if place
were not yielded to the two other antagonistic strongholds, which, if less operative at this precise point of
time, have actually a firmer and more permanent grip
on the prejudices and egoistic impulse of mankind.

The first of these grounds of objection is the one

which all will recognise under the title of the sentimental; the next is the economic. That to which, as
chiefly demanding attention at the present juncture,
I dedicate the largest portion of my space, may be
characterised as the physiological.

It is perhaps lightly assumed that, in view of the
urgency of the struggle for existence in which women
are now largely required to take part, the merely sentimental aspect of this contention might be left to
itself, as admittedly outworn. That such is not the
case a very little reflection will suffice to make clear.
If the reader will consult his memory as to the style
of rhetoric with which he is most familiar in this
matter, whether it reach him in ordinary social intercourse or on the platform, under the sanction of Sanitary Congresses or other associations for the advance-
ment of the public weal, he will be forced to admit
that the sentimental fallacy is still allowed largely to
colour the mass of the thought bestowed upon this
question. I appeal to those persons even who are
moving in the full current of the most plausible
opinion of the hour. Their fortune will have vastly
bettered my own if the lurking desire to retain the
gentler sex as pensioners upon masculine bounty has
not been found to be very dear and deeply rooted in
the manly mind; and that in face of a battle for
life so hard that the would-be dispensers of all material advantages are often unable to keep their own

legs in the struggle. I desire to accord all possible credit to those who would retain the *beau rôle* of benefactors for themselves. Doubtless the sentiment is often sincere, and is then mingled with much of true gentleness. If commonly it is a survival from an earlier and a ruder time, when the attitude of lordly protection was a necessary safeguard of society, at its best it springs from a consideration of the heavier burthens which encumber female effort. Happily so much of the feeling as would do honour to human nature in all times need never pass out of practice; the tenderness which prompts to justice and mercy, when neither can be physically enforced, may exist to-day and to-morrow, as in those dark ages which chivalry enlightened; only it must take on other forms suited to the altered conditions of our crowded modern world. The true paladin of the nineteenth century, the real inheritor of knightly tradition, is he who, sensible of the more ruinous forms of danger and intensified struggle from which man in the aggregate is powerless to protect his helpmate, accepts the new order for her and for himself, and, where he cannot help forward her steps, forbears to harass the progress she is making under the lash of stern necessity.

Now it so happens that the callings which the sentimentalists of the opposite sex are most earnest in tabooing to women, those against which they are most ready to affix the black mark of " unwomanly," are precisely such as offer the highest rewards in money or

consideration. One is tempted to ask if the men, kindly
or hostile, theorists or practitioners, who would push
the weaker vessels from the better-paying spheres of
labour, and so force them to overcrowd the callings
which thus become inadequate to support life, have
thought of any device for getting substitutes to work
for the dispossessed, or of winning them in all cases to
accept such service if found. Where neither worked
for or suffered to work on terms as equal as nature
will permit, to what fate, we would ask, is the woman
to be consigned?

The fair picture, which as a picture we all know so
well (I am about to quote from a recent address), of
"the man going forth to his work and to his labour,
and the woman waiting at home to welcome him back
and lend her ear to his doing or suffering" (with all
the cheerful sympathy of the abundant leisure of, say,
a poor man's wife and mother of his children!), has
lately been recalled to the attention of a large audience,
and reproduced approvingly by the most weighty
organs of the press. If this picture was ever largely
taken from life, it has certainly now little worth as a
truthful representation of the condition of the toiling
masses. That which we look back upon as the age
of chivalry, to a partial view of which it would seem
originally to owe its existence, has long passed, and in
its palmiest hour the queens of beauty, those who,
sitting on high above the heat and dust of the conflict, graced victory with a wreath or a smile, were

few, while the hard-handed Joans and Jills were many,
and more hopelessly underfoot even than the strug-
glers of to-day.

It must surely be acknowledged that none have
such cause to regret the age of chivalry, thus flatter-
ingly conceived, as the women from whose lives despair of the recurrence of its more gracious aspects
has taken not a little of the amenity. The temper of
the sex, as moulded by nature and circumstances, is
not greatly militant; and as a considerable amount of
indolence and inertia is characteristic of human nature
generally, we can hardly err in assuming that the vast
majority of women would still prefer to be sheltered
from, not to say lifted above, the rude battle of life,
and to have their part in it taken by some man to
whom the fight might prove an agreeable stimulant.
But it may not be. If all that has been changed, it
would be well for the sentimentalist to remember that
the change has been effected not so much by women—
certainly not by the rank and file of them—as in their
despite. If in large numbers they are seen to be
pressing forward, and endeavouring to force and to fit
themselves for new spheres of labour, it is not that
their choice lies between work and ease, but between
work and work. No stronghold of prejudice, no earth-
work of selfish interest, could long suffice to withhold
the prizes of labour from an army of workers who are
coming at last to a knowledge of their strength, and
increasing their possession in it from day to day.

The man as the providence of the woman, the woman as the rewarder of labour and strife, is undoubtedly a tempting representation ; but it is condemned as out of keeping with the stern realism of the age. Let us hope that, as a compensation for the loss of this fair dream, some higher form of good, some more potent idea of beauty, may arise out of the hardier conditions which, whether we like them or not, we are compelled to accept. In any case, the more reasonable among women are agreed not to squander time and energy in vain regret for a state of things which no available power could now make to be even a working hypothesis. It is time that the often very clever men, who still flourish the faded banner of chivalry, together with the less reasonable or less vitally interested among women, should copy the resignation of those most deeply concerned, and cease to maintain any figment of argument on grounds of fancy which the hard facts of modern life must often make to seem absurd.

I have spoken of the widening of the sphere of labour for which the sounder education, technical and other, of the women of all ranks is fitting them, but it is easy to overstate the effect of that impulse of extension, as it exists in practice up to the present time, and more particularly in the intellectual sphere. In this country, at least, the higher education has up to this date been mainly instrumental in improving the quality of intellectual effort and the standing of pro-

fessors in the one field (that of instruction of the childhood and youth of their own sex), which has always been
the special, heretofore the sole province, of the quasi-
educated woman.   In proportion to the large numbers
of women who are now annually receiving the benefits
of the higher education, even the medical profession,
for which their natural qualifications would seem in
a marked degree to fit them, has gained fewer recruits
than might perhaps have been expected; and clerk-
ships of all sorts furnish employment at present to a
smaller contingent of Englishwomen than of Americans,
perhaps even—though I have no means of verifying this
—of our neighbours across the water.   It is certainly
wise that steps taken upon unknown ground should
be cautious; and withal, it can safely be affirmed
that the wall of invincible prejudice restricting the
employment of women has given way at many points;
that it lies no longer with a dead-weight upon the
development of their faculties, and that the needy
among them will not in future be condemned to starve
within a charmed circle of hostile opinion.

While on the subject of the sentimental objections
to female progress in new paths, a few words must be
given to those views of Dr. Richardson which saw the
light in the September number of *Longman's Magazine*.   As a physicist speaking to matters of fact, Dr.
Richardson has done such true service in the cause
of those women whose exceptional gifts or common
necessities require of them hard work of body or brain,

that it would be ungrateful to question the good faith
of his intentions throughout. But while this is thank-
fully acknowledged, it would be difficult to point to
any recent utterance, at all authoritative, so well
adapted to reinforce the sentimental fears of the opponents of the movement. Even as the sanitary
cities and dwellings devised by Dr. Richardson must
be found too depressing in their bald ugliness for the
health of the many-sided creature known as man, so
the image presented to us by the same artist of the
woman who has purchased her capacity for toil of
body or mind at the cost of all womanly attributes, is
perilously fitted to be set up at the entrance to the
new fields of labour as a scarecrow.

It is well to know, on the assurance of a physiologist
of Dr. Richardson's standing, that the notions quite
recently current with regard to the congenital incapacity of women for many movements which come
naturally to men and boys, are erroneous, the practical
unskilfulness of the former being the result only of
hereditary disuse of the muscles required to give
effect to such movements. It is when the learned
Doctor exchanges his facts for speculation, and would
bid those who have only just emerged from the clouds
of the past to follow him into the clouds of the future,
that we must decline the invitation, preferring the
passably fair dream that we have lost to the night-
mare with which he would replace it. For little less
terrifying is the picture of a being rendered capable

for strenuous toil by being differentiated body, if not
soul, from the last and most gracious work of Nature.
Dr. Richardson asserts that all motions performed by
men are possible to women. We receive this assurance of solidarity of structure with satisfaction, and
with a sense even of increased power; remembering,
however, that though " all things are lawful, all things
are not convenient." We have a strong persuasion
that it is in other than the fields of physical address
that the highest triumphs of women are to be won.
As to the profession of arms, which he seems to think
applicable to women, beyond a vagrant spirit to be
found among them here and there, the "*ewige weibliche*"
is fundamentally opposed to it; its work in the physical sphere being creative, not destructive, and its
office in the spiritual to save, not to slay.

Those exercises of gymnastic or games of bodily
prowess best suited to maintaining in health, and
assisting the physical development of girls, so far from
being antagonistic to beauty and grace, should be
practised to an extent hitherto unknown in the modern
world to ensure it in full perfection. It would be un-
just, however, to Dr. Richardson to assume that he
would deny the proposition if carried no farther than
this. It is to the excessive muscular development consequent on certain occupations that he alludes. But
for such there can be no need newer than the driving
force of circumstances which have always compelled
certain classes of women to hard bodily labour. With

the effect of this physical strain we are all familiar; but it has never yet been seen to unsex the workers in the manner contemplated by this latest prophet of labour. In some respects it has even approached them nearer to the ideal of womanhood presented in the work of the great Greek masters, than those Dutch doll figures which, in contradistinction, may be called the tailor's ideal, that now harass the sense of beauty at every turn. It might indeed be found that equalised exercise of every function of mind or body, by those in a position to afford attention to such harmonious development, would result in a symmetry somewhat wide even of the best types of the womanhood to which our nineteenth-century eyes are accustomed. There might be a return in nature to the highest ideal in art, wherein the human in man or woman is felt to dominate the merely sexual. So much may be granted; and if this were so, who would dare, in face of the reticent loveliness of the maidens of the Parthenon frieze, to say that the result would be a loss to beauty?

It is probable that strenuous work can hardly be kept up by persons disabled by pressure from filling their lungs with sufficient air; and with the freedom of the waist one chief cause of the excessive emphasis of the bust and hips in modern figures would disappear. I have no doubt that the loss, if it were general, would be much lamented, and the forms so toned down held to be insipid by misguided dilettanti of the sex that has long obtained freedom for itself. The eye that has been over-stimulated, like a palate accustomed to highly-seasoned dishes, would require time to recover its normal sensibility; but, if change we must have, it would almost seem that it must now come to us in the direction of sobriety, the outlines at present in vogue being too elephantine to be capable of much increase.

Dr. Richardson seems to think that some considerable number of women will in the future elect to follow callings which, from the loss of charm which they exact, and from other reasons, will definitely exclude them from wifehood and maternity—all, in fact, which has hitherto been the dearest hope of the majority of the sex. I must think that the reckoning has in this case been made without the human heart, and those various and complex sentiments it is apt to draw into its service; and that the omission vitiates all the terms of the problem. There will never, to begin with, be such an order of uncloistered, unprofessed, and self-devoted nuns as is here contemplated by Dr. Richardson; and further, although the classes with low cerebral development renew their kind more rapidly than those of higher nervous nature, and although nervous force of any description extended over a wider area may take something from fecundity, the human creature is too many-sided for the customary daily work, which engages but a portion of its energy, to modify the organism to the point which Dr. Richardson's view implies. It may be true that genius, which is as a double rose, has few heirs in the flesh and none in the spirit; but genius is of rare apparition, and takes little account of our transitory arrangements, and we on our part may afford to leave it to its own devices. It is with the commoner flower of human faculty that we have to do. Not while there is warmth enough left in the old earth to kindle a match will the working woman, we may be very sure, be reduced to the condition of the working bee. What the case may be thought to prove in regard to the physical status of the offspring of women, hard-worked either in brain or body, I reserve for consideration in its place farther on.

But the anticipated material loss, that of beauty and fertility, on the part of the toiling woman, is only a portion of that which weighs on the future she is called to face with such courage as she can command. She has continually to hear that all which has hitherto constituted her inward grace and charm, her capacity to bring solace and delight to her mate and co-worker of the other sex, is fatally imperilled, not only by her efforts towards honourable independent existence, if a single life should become her portion, but also by the fuller culture which in any progressive state of society could alone maintain her as the companion of man. And this fear of loss through the sounder education of women is by no means confined to the hard, the grudging, or the unbelieving of the opposite sex. It is to be met with in the tender, the generous, and most

B

hopeful of those who reckon upon the joint influence
of women in the amelioration of the worst evils of life.
What is more common than to hear from the lips of
men full of reverence for womanhood, as they conceive
of it, that the attractive spontaneity which now distinguishes the sex would be impaired by the cultivation
of the reasoning faculty, and that the love of rule so
proper to the masculine mind would be in danger of
coming into more active collision with a partner who
had learnt to think as well as to feel? Perhaps of all
the strongholds which sentiment still maintains, this,
which keeps possession of the border and claims to be
protecting, is the most difficult to invade. And yet
it ought not to be hard of proof that the assumptions
on which it stands are ill-founded. Surely a little
power of logical conclusion should be held no hin-
drance to what is regarded, with a subtle mixture of
flattery and contempt, as the airy flight of women's
thought. If the impulsive method of reaching its
ends, believed to be distinctive of the female mind, is
really inherent in that little-understood organ, and if
it is thus better fitted for sympathetic contact with
that of the male, nature may be trusted to its own
devices for guarding a quality really worthy of per-
petuation. There will be no need to cripple female
intelligence in order to induce it to take or return
to its native mode of propulsion. If it be not profane
to say so, the manner of its movement hitherto has had
in it something too much of the *kite*, liable to be caught

and blown about by every casual wind; it would be a
great thing if a large part of what has been merely
accidental and external were exchanged for the pur-
posive in its action.   If women's thoughts are to be
conceived of as winged, while those of men have hands
and feet, let them at least share with the bird something besides its impatience of walking the earth.   It
is beyond a doubt that the feathered tribe are conscious
of the more striking of the features of the landscape
over which they pass, know, for instance, whether their
flight is taken over land or sea, or even over mountain
and forest.   Let the kindly sentimentalist of the opposite sex take the bird, and not the paper toy, for the
admired type, and allow that it may be well for a
woman to know something of the ground of an argument, even if she have flown at the conclusion.

With respect to the second of the two contingencies
feared by the admirers of the *gentle* sex, I believe it to
be a bugbear with even less of substance than the
foregoing.   It is more than probable that a well-trained
mind will acquire independent vigour, and thus be better
prepared to hold its own on abstract questions of morals,
politics, or art; but I confidently appeal to observers
of human life to negative the assumption, that in the
concrete of everyday practice the more reasonable of
any two married partners is the one who may be expected to rule the day in a war of wills.   So little is
this the case, that a sensible decline of female influence
in the outer sphere might with greater justice be appre-

hended from the abandonment of the methods of defence
or attack resorted to in acknowledged weakness and
hopeless inferiority.

The world has never yet been ruled by reason; and
of all creatures, next to a child new-born, a reasonable
woman may be regarded as the most unfended. As-
piring to be the friend of her husband; with love too
pure for treachery where love survives; scorning to
steal her way by the back-stairs of his vanity and
weakness when it has departed; too proud in conscious worth, it must also be said, to wait, a cringing
courtier, in the ante-chamber of his moods; without
hysterics as a set-off against the violence of masculine
temper, she has no armour but her truth, no sword
but of the spirit. We may hope that the faith in
good of the free soul of educated woman will be justified in the end; but for the moment, with public
opinion half-hearted and the law as an adversary, her
position is full of trial, and even of danger. If these
words appear startling and the picture overdrawn, it
will only be to those who live in forgetfulness that a
mother who has not broken her marriage pledge can
still be deprived of her children (the most naturally
inviolable of all human possessions) by other hand
than that of death. Such a consideration is well calculated to make the educated and thoughtful pause
before placing themselves in possible danger of a law
so inhuman. In the freest nation under the sun, the
England of to-day, there is no security of freedom or

justice for the married woman, who is essentially bond according to the flesh, though as God's free agent and minister she may be taking a share in human progress not the less important because unacknowledged.

In any case, those who, from whatever cause, delight in the contemplation of woman as a dependent on man, have no need to fear a reversal of this order as the result of an education whose tendency is to deprive the weaker vessel of the grosser earthly means and selfish cunning which have been the resource of enslaved spirits in all ages. As I have endeavoured to show, it is highly probable that education, in taking the fetters from the soul and supplying a higher ideal of wifely duty, will add to, rather than diminish, the pliancy of woman in her external relations to man as his companion and helpmate.

PART II.

*IN WHICH THE ECONOMIC PROBLEM IS
EXAMINED.*

II.

IN reviewing the current objections to the more active part which women are now taking in the work of the world under its second head, that which I have called the economic, we come to a widely different class of facts. In the sentimental fallacy we have had to do with ideas whose manifestation has been very vague and cloudy, while the assertion of them is made openly, in the proud confidence of views not formed to discredit the holder. With the objections on the economic side the reverse of this obtains. The underlying facts are hard—as stony and impenetrable as crude self-interest can make them ; but this stony core is concealed by pretentious arguments, often specious, rarely sincere ; always and wholly untrustworthy.

The active if unavowed principle in this portion of the contention is the desire on the part of the male worker to keep the labour market free, if not wholly of the concurrence, at least of the skilled concurrence of women. Men have been accustomed from the beginning of civilisation to see women taking up the fag-ends of work, and spending and squandering strength, and deadening life and hope in untrained effort; and this they are prepared to endure complacently to the end. But to have them competing for the higher rewards of cultivated faculty has proved too much for the justice, to say nothing of the " chivalry," not indeed of individual men, but of men in the aggregate. That this is so has been shown of recent years in many a calling, high and low, which has become a guild for the exclusion of the weaker sex. There is need for open-speaking on this matter, but I am too reluctant to stir up bitter memories to do more than glance in passing at the trials experienced at the hands of a clique of professors and more shameless undergraduates by medical women in Edinburgh, and the hostility, carried almost to the length of personal assault, of the representatives of various trades which the labours of women have from time to time invaded.

First in plausibility among the arguments by which the progress of women in quality of work, whether intellectual or merely manual, is opposed, we may count that which assumes that for every woman who wins a place in the ranks of intelligent or otherwise skilled labour, some one man who, if her hands were tied, might be her bread-winner, is ousted.

This plea would be not only plausible, but tenable, if there were an equal number of marriageable men and women, and every man were compelled by law to take a wife, every woman a husband. As it is, with the vast numbers of marriageable men abroad or otherwise unavailable, and with the greater nicety of choice which a higher order of culture tends to induce in women, it means only that the woman shall have the first chance of any prospect of starvation which may happen to be on foot. To whatever end it may be held to work, marriage, looked upon as a natural means of provision for a girl, and the sole means of her rise in life, does, and must continue in increasing measure to pass from the calculations of young women whose faculties are rejoicing in congenial exercise. The husbands who win them, with a risk of turning aside from definite interests or an absorbing career, may, without fatuity, entertain some comfortable assurance in regard to the nature of the sentiment which has secured their conquest. If qualifications other than those of householder and purse-bearer are likely to become more largely in request, such a raising of the standard of requirement could not be hurtful to society.

The period in semi-civilised life when it could be assumed that a woman, or more often a child, was bound in duty to take the husband of her parents' selection, and be content to be given into his hands in exchange for value received, is happily past. The woman at her present point of progress is making more than the step beyond this primitive state at which her course was for some time arrested. She is asserting her right to rebel, not alone against the tyranny of human will, but against all that is preventable in the tyranny of circumstances. As I have said, there is a feeling arising among young women that they will no

longer be forced upon marriage as the only means and
end of existence. The delicate instincts of that true
womanhood which can only be evolved in freedom,
shrink from the fact of union on any other basis than
that of personal sympathy as from an odious violation.
This being the case, though every man who might
owe his professional success to the absence of female
concurrence should feel it his duty to take to himself
and to provide for one of those who should be bound
in his interest to swell the ranks of the " unemployed,"
a large contingent of the best and purest would remain,
thrown back upon a state of existence in which all hope
of independence, all reasonable ambition, was denied
them.

During the last few decades a considerable amount
of female energy has been set free from the drudgery
of domestic work. This has been most felt in the
higher, middle, and professional classes, where there
has been a growing feeling on the part of the
daughters, for whom scant provision is generally
made, that the time reserved to them by labour-
saving inventions—as, for instance, the sewing-machine
and the manufacture on a large scale of articles of
food and clothing*—may well be employed in ensuring
the means of independent existence. The members of
this considerable class refuse to be reduced to the condition of a Grand Llama in all but its security and
honour, and stand, and will stand, by their right to a

* See Mrs. Henry Sedgwick on the University Education of Women.

place, and as good a place as their abilities can justify, in the army of labour. If we are told that there is not work enough for both sexes, or wage enough to pay the workers so that they can live by their toil, that is no good reason for making an arbitrary choice as to which of them shall live and which shall starve. Still less is it a reason for giving the preference to the weaker vessel in such an election.

Our cumulative difficulty of over-population presents many aspects which cannot here be gone into. It is to be feared that difficulty can only be met (until moral feeling is more advanced than it is likely to be for many generations) by emigration or colonisation on a larger scale than has ever yet been contemplated; and as pioneers of labour in the rough conditions of early settlement, no one will question that men are better fitted than the more physically burthened and weaker sex.

A more valid plea for the restriction of female labour than the foregoing is one which applies only to those women who have passed from the celibate condition to that of wife and mother. That loss to the home may be presumed from the absence of its mistress, whether engaged in professional pursuits, in washing, charing, factory-work, or any other, no one will attempt to deny. But the frequent necessity for such double charge is unfortunately no new thing, more especially in our crowded manufacturing centres. Such cases are hard upon the woman and child, and,

by reflection, upon the man.   Hard upon the woman,
because her energies, if not greatly beyond the common,
are overtaxed by daily work in addition to the cares
and sorrows inevitable to her condition and sex.   It is
clear, therefore, that it is only under the pressure of
necessity that a woman willingly takes upon herself
such twofold burthens.   Where the earning power of
the husband suffices, and where proved exceptional
gifts have not brought with them the responsibility of
exercise, there is no call for the concurrence of the
wife as a bread-winner.   That the labour of the husband does not oftener suffice is due in far greater
degree to early and improvident marriages, wherein
boys and girls, often in their teens, come together
without care or thought of the future, than to the
part which women are claiming in honest labour, however skilful or intelligent.

In turning our thoughts in this connection to the
intellectual class, it may be said that the husband and
children of a professional woman would be less likely
to suffer from the withdrawal of a portion of her time
from her home duties than are those of the ordinary
woman of fashion, whose proceedings we are all accustomed to witness, and generally without protest or
cry of alarm.   The better-educated conscience of the
former might confidently be expected to lead to greater
care in the appointment of substitutes, or rather of
subordinates ; and her trained intelligence might generally be relied on for the establishment of a better

method for their practice and more enlightened super-
vision of its results.

A third objection on the economic side to that
advanced education, whether intellectual or merely
technical, which is fitting women for the more paying
pursuits, is founded on the assumption of their radical
incapacity to turn knowledge, even when acquired, to
adequate practical account. It is perhaps seldom that
we hear the case so crudely stated; but the little importance attached by most men, and many women, to
the upheaval which is going on all around us, is
silently eloquent of the contempt which a force wholly
spiritual still meets in a world which continues to be
governed by "big battalions." If now and again this
commonly silent scorn finds utterance, it is when the
battle has waxed hot, and some antagonist of female
endeavour is driven to his last defences. We are then
told that time and money are unprofitably expended
in any serious apprenticeship of a creature for whose
use the differential calculus must ever remain an instrument too subtle, and who has never yet gifted the
world with an important discovery in science or a *chef
d'œuvre* in art. The list of these sins of omission is
unending, as the register which Leporello unfolds of his
master's loves. Women have played with the ivory
keys for centuries, and have written no great music.
(This is a stock indictment.) They have cooked for
the universe, and never yet invented a dish. They
have—— But I forbear from further variation of the

theme. If the charge were true in every particular, which may fairly be denied, it would prove nothing in the case now on its trial of woman *versus* man, wherein it is only claimed by the former that she shall be allowed such a share as she can prove herself capable of performing in the world's common and daily work.

For the above ground of objection to have any just weight, it should be shown that the average man, the great mass of those who have in all ages enjoyed educational advantages withheld from the other sex, is generally endowed with the qualities which all women are said to lack. That this is not the case is a matter calling for no proof; original genius is rare as the bluebird, though its effects are not unfrequently counterfeited by the ingenious chemistry of well-instructed talent. And it is perhaps to the advantage of the world that it should be so. It is desirable that a lightning flash shall illumine the scene occasionally, but a well-trimmed lamp is a thing more easy of control. Perhaps no great effective loss would result were women found to be indeed incapable of yielding the more erratic light. One such electric flash is sufficient to kindle a whole field of science, and set a thousand plodding workers in their places, gathering together the scattered portions of a treasure so revealed. The management of the world's affairs is clumsy enough as it is, but it is nothing to the confusion worse confounded which would result if its details were confided in practice to the exalted geniuses whose capacity to cast light into the dark places of natural fact and of human thought is maintained by a power of abstraction, a disengagement from external surroundings, which commonly leaves them in all that relates to dealing with men and things in the helpless innocence of childhood.

Since the above position can hardly be controverted, I think to have shown that the special originative power so imperatively denied to women is a faculty wholly unneeded in any attempt to make good their present claim; but withal I cannot forbear a word or two of protest from what may, even in this advanced age of the world, be regarded as a pre-judgment of feminine limitations.

Of all the charges of inferiority on which the changes are rung, the incapacity of women for musical composition appears to be the favourite. The sex has never given to the world a great musical composer. Now it seems to me that the superior attitude assumed when this assertion is made is unwarranted. True, the foremost musical names are of the other sex, but we shall have to acknowledge, on looking into the register for all time, that the list is, in comparison with that of the sister arts, a quite remarkably short one.

It is further asserted that the absence of women's names from the muster roll of great musicians is the more significant because more women than men have

C

been students of this art. If this statement may not
be wholly denied, it is necessary to correct it at the
outset by saying that it applies only to later times, and
chiefly, even thus, to our own country. But further
than this, it can be proved to be positively untrue that,
of those who have made of music a serious study even
in England and of recent years, the majority have been
women. That girls in large numbers have been taught,
whether with the grain or against it, to dally with the
keys or strings, is true enough; it has been a part of
the " accomplishment " which has been supposed to fit
them for their dependent function; but this is not the
way in which the men who have set their lives apart
to the service of a most exacting art have prepared
themselves for their vocation. We learn that of Men-
delssohn and his sister, Fanny had the finer musical
organisation, and was supposed to offer the greater
promise, until their training, which had been the same
up to a certain point, diverged; or rather, when that
of the girl, impeded by the dead-weight of customary
opinion, was stopped short, while that of the boy was
encouraged and assisted in its advance. It is only those
who have penetrated no farther than to the threshold
of musical science who can imagine that the construction of great works is an affair simply of imaginative
impulse. It needs but a glance at the " Lives " of
musical composers to assure us that the high gift,
generally hereditary, almost always fostered by active
care and congenial surroundings, exacts for its full

fruition a degree of detachment from the common concerns of life which would be sufficient in itself to over-
whelm the solicitous soul of woman with the obloquy
it would be sure to bring upon her. And this cannot
be otherwise while anything of the Oriental and generally obscurantist conception of the destiny of woman
as subservient to man prevails.

It is no part of my purpose in this essay to insist
on the possible equality of the sexes on the supposition
of an equality of conditions; I am rather seeking to
draw such conclusions as are practicable from facts as
I find them at the moment.

In the entanglement of human motive, however
much or little may be conceded to honest conservative
feeling in regard to the enlarged sphere of activity
now claimed by women, it must be allowed that the
real tug of war, the utmost bitterness of invective,
begins only with the cheapening of the market. As
might be predicted, this inimical feeling is deepest, if
more restrained in expression, in those higher intellectual spheres where there is most to lose or gain; but
every calling upon which the pressure of bitter need
has forced an entrance to women has found irate and
powerful defenders. And all the more, possibly, in
that the lesser physical needs or exactions of women
enable them to work for poorer pay. That the current price of women's work should be less, say, on an
average, by one-half than that of men, is a fact which
is everywhere acquiesced in. There are many causes

besides the above which contribute to this result. I
have taken some trouble to arrive at, and to test, the
nature, essential or merely accidental, of some of these;
but the task is not easy. So much of passion and prejudice distorts the so-called *facts*, that for any working
value that is left in them they are little better than
falsehoods. With all that class of debaters who regard women as radically inferior in faculty from first
to last, the one and efficient cause assigned for poor
pay is the poorness of the service rendered. That
women's work in every department even of industry
is and must be poor, is a canonised assumption with
this considerable party, and one from which they draw
their texts. It is averred * that even in sewing, their
one speciality, if they were capable of maintaining it,
they are everywhere and necessarily outdone by men.
Now this is a tangible proposition, relating to matters
as they are seen to exist, and one of which, even in the
present state of inferior technical training bestowed
upon female children, it is easy to prove the mendacity.
We will take needlework in what every one who has
used a needle knows to be its most difficult product
(needle-wrought lace alone excepted), viz., fine satin-
stitch embroidery and open work. The case as between
the hereditary male embroiderers of Indian muslin, and
to some minor extent the also hereditary embroideresses
of French cambric, will be acknowledged as a fair
example, or, if not quite fair, one certainly not erring

* *Vide* a recent article in the *Spectator*.

by being more advantageous to the female side of the question. I appeal then to any one competent to form a judgment on the matter (one of the few on which I should not hesitate myself to become a juror), as to whether the work of the Frenchwomen (chiefly shepherdesses), does not surpass in all that constitutes high technical merit that of the Indian workers in the same field. That it does surpass it I boldly take for fact, upon the basis of which we have a right to assume that, given equal advantages to the tailoresses, they could certainly hold their own against the tailors. In urging this, I put forward no high intellectual claim, unprovable in the present experimental stage of affairs. Even as regards tailoring, I confine myself to that part of the work which comes under the head of sewing. As I have said, it is difficult to make one's way through the mass of distorted evidence that encumbers every branch of the question of woman's fitness for work in competition with men, and my means of acquiring information have not been the same in every department even of this particular industry; but I would suggest to those who are better informed the inquiry as to what proportion the training of the women-tailors bears to the long apprenticeship of men; and also the reflection that, seeing the miserable earnings of the former, how much insufficient nourishment may be chargeable with the possible absence of the modicum of physical strength needed for some portions of the performance.

I own there was a time when I myself succumbed
to some discouragement in accepting the assurance that
the female hand was incompetent to the perfecting of
a button-hole. I have since, in frequent disproof, seen
reason to smile at my easy admission of so palpable an
absurdity; but indeed I had more cause to blush. I
had long known that women were the makers of the
lace, the *point d'Alençon*, of which I was an amateur,
and considered myself a judge. As every one knows,
the button-hole stitch, in its various applications and in
different degrees of tension, is the basis of this lace,
made with a flaxen thread so fine that the damp air of
a cellar is needed to keep it from breaking while mani-
pulated by that instrument of precision, the wondrously
tactile female hand. Those of my readers who have
looked at this utmost product of delicate human skill
through a strong lens, will know that a square inch of
the fabric may be magnified to four times its size and
yet appear fine, and with every stitch as fairly set as
if it had been worked in bobbin. Truly, in comparison
with such fairy-work, the button-holes which we have
feebly suffered to be thrown in our faces might be
thought to have been cobbled by gnomes.*

I will not weary my reader by dwelling upon facts
which have become commonplaces in this discussion.
It is known, or should be known, to all, from frequent
repetition, that in all matters of simple acquirement,

* It may not be irrelevant to note in this place that women are
paid twopence a day, in some cases less, for the working of button-
holes.

competing women have won for themselves such a
place as is likely materially to stimulate the exertions
of men, and that without the advantage of a single generation of hereditary preparation. Where one woman
has given proof of such mathematical capacity as to
put male Wranglers on their best metal, and where
another, in a mixed examination of the most " excru-
ciating kind," has come out against her male compe-
titors with what are called " honours of the first class,"
it may be confidently expected that the veriest fogies
seeking shelter from the current of progress in the back-
waters of conservatism will awake to the fallacy of any
argument based on the incapacity of women to deal
with numerals or to acquire scholarship.* It may be
urged that the possession of the above faculties does
not imply the organising power needed for the conduct
of the higher affairs of life ; but I am not aware that
the latter, which is seen in germ in every well-ordered
household, and is at the root of all social success, has
ever been proved wanting to the female half of the race ;
and certainly their conduct of such public business,
philanthropic or other, as has hitherto fallen to their
share has afforded no warrant of inefficiency. I know
of American women who are the successful managers
of large farms, and every traveller in Europe is acquainted with hotels of which women are the indefati-
gable heads. It is, I believe, less known, it was, at least,

* The above was written before the question received further illumi-
nation from the achievements of Miss Ramsay of Girton and Miss
Hervey of Newnham.

new to me when I learnt it of Dr. Richardson, that
women have recently attained success in a sphere of
labour to which they have heretofore been strangers:
that of practical mechanicians. I cannot do better
than quote his words :—

" In the course of the present year I visited a factory
where women were at work before the lathe, the vice,
the anvil, making parts of important and delicate
machinery in steel, iron, and brass. They were white-
smiths, turners, and brass-finishers. Struck with so
novel a sight, I spent an hour in the shops with them,
looking at the works they carried out, and I am bound
to say that better and truer workmanship I never beheld. The dexterity with which those who worked with
the hammer used that instrument; their correctness of
eye in measuring minute distances and irregularities,
the rapidity with which they turned out work from the
lathe, and the ease and accuracy with which they collected and put the various parts together in order to
complete the instruments they were producing, was a
new study to me, sufficient of itself to correct the early
and incorrect impressions I had acquired, if nothing
else in the way of evidence had been brought under
my observation. There was no exhibit in these workers
of any deficiency of muscular perception or skill. Everything done was decisively done, quickly done, accurately
done, and strongly done." In some muscular work it is
even asserted by Dr. Richardson that women have, from
their construction, an advantage over men. If they do

not stand as firmly as men, they sit more firmly, and thus have the power of using their lower limbs with greater effect.

The above is trustworthy evidence, and easily verifiable by any one in whose unwilling mind there still exists a doubt; and what, in the face of it, becomes of the argument which turns upon the waste of time and money incurred in educating the uneducable?

I am not aware what proportion the wages received by the skilled workwomen whose performance so interested Dr. Richardson may have borne, or may still be bearing, to that of the men they compete with; but however it may be in their special case, it is at least sure that in their thorough training and accomplishment they are opening out the road to their less capable, because less instructed, sisters, by which they can alone hope to maintain fair terms for their labour, even if something may be done on other lines towards relieving the generally grinding oppression of the famine prices at which their work is at present rated. Sound work, the preparation for which should be given in schools where technical knowledge forms a prominent part of the teaching, and association for mutual support can be the only remedies for this inequality. This matter of association, to which the whole history of women's past has tended to disincline them, is second in importance only to that of completer technical training, and calls for serious consideration and prompt effort on the part of the organisers of labour. That without it even technical efficiency fails in most departments to obtain anything like equality of pay is clear to all who have cared to make the inquiry. As mistress of a household, I feel myself again on familiar ground when I point to the colourable superstition which existed but a decade or so ago, to the effect that female domestic service was inadequate to the satisfactory performance of all that was necessary to a well-mounted establishment. It was confidently believed and asserted by mistresses that no woman could clean and keep silver plate as it was cleaned and kept by men; it was an article of faith that the mysteries of the cellar were unfathomable by a female butler; and it was expected that the waitresses who served at table should be as hair-brained and as liable to accident as Hebe herself. Now all this is changed. Prejudice and love of show, or what is known as "style," apart, in this department women have clearly beaten men out of the field. They undertake and do more work, and the performance of a well-trained parlour-maid fully equals that of the male servant, even in the keeping of the plate, which was so lately regarded as his speciality. As butlers, women have the great advantage that their knowledge of the liquors under their care more commonly remains theoretic; and as waiters, their lighter motions and more silent service especially commend them. Judged of fairly all round, I hardly think that any housekeeper who has had experience of both would hesitate, as regards domestic service, to give the palm to women

over men. And yet here the same anomaly faces us
that we have encountered elsewhere, with this difference, that here, having the case in full light before us,
we are not led to charge the fact on any radical inferiority in the work rendered. The anomaly to which
I would draw attention is, that the market value of
women's service in this department, as in others, is
less, often less than half, that of men. Of course it
may be urged, and with truth, that this is due to the
greater pressure of female candidates for places. I only
cite the fact in proof that here at least, where the case
lies near at hand for scrutiny, it is not the lower
quality of the labour which causes the difference ; and
inferentially the same may apply to other female
industries of which we have not the same means of
judging.

Much, therefore, as may be hoped in regard to the
condition of working-women from a more extensive
and perfected technical training, it will be seen that
there exists a strong necessity for supplementing this
by those means of combined action which, as exercised
by the male worker, have done, and are still doing, so
much towards that more equal distribution of wealth
which is erroneously regarded by the too highly privileged classes as a decline in national prosperity.

That female labour in almost every province is
wretchedly ill-paid, is a fact so familiar that it has
come to be treated with the proverbial contempt. But
as one of the most fruitful sources of human misery

and degradation, its call for helpful effort on the part
of those who have the welfare of their kind at heart can
never cease to be imperative. M. Felix Remo, in his
highly suggestive work "*L'Egalité des Sexes*," demands,
with the epigrammatic neatness characteristic of French
writers, the reason of this "violation of the economic
formula : for equal product, equal pay." He affirms it
to be pretended that men have families to support, and
then asks if that has ever been recognised as a ground
of difference in the salaries of married and single men?
"Even if it were," he adds, " are there no women with
families to support? and they at least (with rare exceptions which fall upon society) do not abandon the
children, too often shaken off or repudiated by their
fathers. And then the widows. In the last census,
of 879,173 widows, nearly two-thirds belonged to the
working-class."

The notion that wages are awarded according to
need may be held to be too fanciful for serious dispute.
Not even in logical France could the pretension to so
nice an adjustment of economic relations be maintained; but in refuting the attempted justification of the
inferior wage of women by their inferior work, M. Remo
furnishes many facts which are of high value in this
discussion. Quoting from the *Bee-Hive* of the 25th
of January 1874, he says that "in the fabrication of
cigars, the best of the produce (of the tobacco-fields) is
confided to men. When, however, as often happens,
the clever workmen fail at their post, recourse is had

to the women, who do their part not only equally
well, but more expeditiously, and are paid, notwithstanding, forty per cent. less than the male workers
they temporarily replace."

Enough has probably been said to satisfy the thoughtful reader, if not already awake to the fact, that while
it is of supreme importance that the technical education of girls should be extended and perfected, other
influences than such as can be ascribed to inefficient
instruction are at work to keep down the wages of
female labour. To particularise all of these would
carry me beyond the limits prescribed to this study.
It will be sufficient to state that the woman-worker,
standing alone and unaided, is beset on every side
with difficulty, if not with injustice and exaction. In
certain callings, that, for instance, of the milliner, a
money deposit is claimed for work executed at home,
and that often in excess of the value of the materials.
In a meeting held at Bristol against this and other abuses,
it was ascertained that a single manufacturer had obtained of his hands, deposits to the value of £3000.

Not only is the unfortunate woman compelled by the
requirements of her family to work at home, ground
down to famine wages, but the middleman, who is ordi-
narily a sort of taskmaster and shopkeeper together, requires that she shall take out the miserable pittance of
her labour in articles of food and clothing, on which his
profits are often exorbitant, and of the bad quality of
which she stands too much in his power to complain.

The under-paid "assistants" in certain shops are compelled, for the honour and glory of the establishment, to wear silk dresses, which taking an undue portion of their pay, they are often driven to eke out their existence in a manner to which the temptation stands only too near.　A letter from the Rev. —— Horsley, chaplain to the Clerkenwell prison, is given by M. Remo in that work above-mentioned, to which I am indebted for many of these details, and I venture to reproduce it as weighty with personal knowledge :—

"It is useless to insist on the temptation to crime and to prostitution which is the consequence of insufficient wages.　The least of the evils which beset the sempstress is the temptation to pawn the work confided to her, together with the coverings and other articles of her poverty-stricken dwelling.　I ardently hope that success may crown your efforts to introduce organisation into women's work, to raise them out of their despair, and afford help to their ignorance in combating the jealousy and selfishness of male workers, and the farming of their labours by that tribe of intermediaries who are nourished at their expense."

This, then, is the point to which all inquiry into the justly remunerative conditions of the labour of at least that portion of the sex which is the poorest and most helpless, must carry us.　Trade-unions, such as abound for men, supplementing a more perfect technical training, are the sorely needed remedies for the evils which beset the unassisted efforts of women. Of the nature and the amount of work which is waiting for such institutions to perform on their behalf, the following fact will afford a fair sample. I translate again from the evidence adduced in "*L'Egalité des Sexes :*"—

"In the course of a single year the union for the protection of the workwomen of New York had to institute proceedings against 160 employers, who, under false pretexts, had reduced or altogether held back the already pitiful pay of their workwomen." Again, "At the time of the recent turn-out of the cotton-spinners of Belfast, men and women, to the number of many thousands, protested by the cessation of work against the diminution of their wages. The men, thanks to their union, succeeded in decreasing by one-half the reduction proposed, while the women, who had no such union, were compelled to accept it entire."

Women even more than men have need of the protection which association can alone afford. A man in his own strength may hold out with no worse a prospect than that of slow starvation. For him there is temptation in many forms, it is true, but not that one gulf darker than death ever open to women in the weakness and dizziness of despair. It is for them that there exists the fatal attraction of a precipice, approached by degrees as over the rounded brow of a hill, which ultimately yawns and plunges the victim into a pit of such horror as has no parallel in the life of any other of God's creatures.

The following are a few of the aids which would accrue to women through association :—

> Help in times of crisis and commercial depression.
>
> Facility of information in regard to the labour market, and the wages in different localities.
>
> Safeguard against the accumulation of labour at any one point.
>
> Encouragement given to a high quality of work by the maintenance of a standard of excellence.
>
> Succour to the sick, together with the comfort and moral force arising from the sense of human relation and sympathy, &c., &c.

It might be supposed that benefits so unquestionable, of which I am far from having exhausted the list, might be safely trusted to commend themselves; but, as I have already indicated, the whole course of life, the whole dependent past of women, has been such as to render them averse to united action among themselves; and it may be justly feared that, until this disinclination, or, where not positive disinclination, inertia has been overcome, the progress of the movement already inaugurated by philanthropists must be slow.

The first union for the protection of working-women from the exactions of employers had birth in New York as far back as 1871. We are told that the president, formerly a working-woman, won the confidence and gratitude of all by the admirable ability displayed in developing and governing the association. Wages have steadily risen, and there have been no more "turnouts." The union is rich, and the sick and those without work are generously aided.

This first union in New York was followed in London, at some little distance of time, by the Woman's Protective and Provident League, founded by Mrs. Paterson, with the advantage of possessing Mrs. Fawcett as permanent president of its meetings. To this, various other unions for the protection of special industries have succeeded, both in London and the provinces.

It is in vain, if it were not worse than vain, that Acts of Parliament should regulate the hours of work. The working-women are aware of the disadvantage under which legal limitation places them, and unscrupulous employers disobeying the law would stand in little fear of being denounced by those whose keenest desire is that their services shall be retained at any price.

It is association, therefore, which can alone be looked to for effective protection. We have seen that such societies are already at work amongst us, but it is to be regretted that they are yet far from having enlisted adherents in numbers commensurate with the benefits they offer. It is clearly not enough that helpful souls from without the industrial ranks should have organised these societies; in order that their advantages should be fully enjoyed, it is above all

D

needful that the perceptions of women and girls shall
be open to their recognition. I naturally conclude
that the subject has been touched from time to time in
lectures delivered to working women, but I think that
a ground should be laid for the enforcement of the
lesson in all schools established for girls of the industrial class. Those who have to gain their living by the
labour of their hands should be left to no haphazard
acquaintance with the means best fitted to ensure
success in a struggle of such difficulty.

In reviewing cursorily this wide subject of women
in their new relation to work, it is difficult to preserve
anything like order.   Not only is one called in turn
to touch upon different rounds of the social ladder, but
the subject is found to overlap at almost every point.
If there is any gain to compensate this loss of method,
it is that each one of its phases has a tendency to illus-
trate the rest.   In my recent remarks I have endeavoured to show proof of the capacity of women as well
in the operative as in the more strictly intellectual
classes for the higher and more remunerative forms of
labour.   Doubtless the hierophants, the men who, like
a priestly or kingly order, would retain the high
privilege of freedom of development for their own half
of the race, would in all cases, but more especially in
such as trenched upon their material interests, show
themselves no less eager to restrain the weaker sex
from advanced technical than from advanced intellectual training. They would say that such training was

thrown away upon beings incapable of scientific method ;
and so far as in them lay, they would take care that
they should remain incapable. But if the economic
results in the higher intellectual sphere are still held
by any competent observers to be doubtful, they can
assuredly not be claimed to be so in the industrial.
Happily the women operatives have taken their case
into their own hands in numbers sufficient to cast shame
on the arrogant assertions of an interested class. As
watchmakers, practical mechanicians, printers, book-
binders, and a variety of other employments calling for
accuracy and intelligence, they have shown themselves
as expert as men wherever their advantages have been
equal; and have proved to their own satisfaction, which
is the point of most importance (since from this the rest
must follow), that they are capable of more intelligent
labour than has heretofore been allotted to them, and
that such labour is remunerative. The case of the
women claiming advanced intellectual culture as a
means of bread-winning is more involved in theory
and not yet so fully established in practice; but the
side-light deflected upon it from the experience of their
humbler sisters is not without significance.

In the zeal of a certain class of men (and the women
who live to please them) for what, while they prefer
to represent it as the well-being of the weaker sex, has
sufficient likeness to an egoistic policy of obscurantism
to justify me in touching on it in this place, utterance
has been given to the notion that bread-earning women

of all classes, the upper no less than the lower, would
do well to confine themselves to the daintier kinds of
manual labour when not engaged in the blind leading
of the blind of their own sex which was once known
as education. Now I will not attempt to deny that
the gain in mental vigour of a merely technical teaching of which the standard is high must be greater than
that of a purely intellectual one of which the standard
is low; but I have difficulty in bringing myself to
stoop to the notice of a proposition which would claim
one-half of the Western world as victims of a system of
" caste," from which even the somnolent East is shaking
itself free.

The possession of mankind in knowledge is increasing hour by hour; and a bar put to the advance of one
sex while the other is being swept forward in the
cumulative speed of the current, would be fatal to that
homogeneous action which is the best hope of the race.
An ever-widening gulf would be set between the sexes,
and it needs no prophet to predict that the curse of
sterility, a state fixed and inert like that which exists
in the East, would fall upon a people who so violated
the natural conditions of development. We have seen
the effects of this divorce, and may see them still, in
the sullen pools which progress has failed to stir, and
must be blind indeed if we do not gather from it that
the same law of sexual contact which prevails in the
material sphere, is equally potent in the spiritual.

For the rest, if the hierophants had their way—of

which there is happily no chance—and if in the division
of labour the lower forms of it with the lower rewards
should increasingly accrue to women (a result which
would be sure to follow the withdrawal of a common
standard for either sex), we might as well at once make
over to the dominant side, the one quasi-intellectual
calling left to us. Not long would women retain their
present position as the instructors of the youth of either
sex. Human beings are so constituted as to be unable
to put forth their best strength unless in reaching
towards some ideal point. The rebuke of hope would
thus vitiate the endeavours of women from the outset.
It would come to be felt that even in the education of
an inferior " caste," such limited knowledge as was
thought proper to them should be sound of its kind,
and that however short the stage they were suffered to
journey, their steps should be set upon the right way
and supported by adequate help ; and thus we may
be sure that, wherever means permitted, recourse would
be had, even in the education of girls, to the qualified
guidance of the master-mind.

In view of the facts I have here brought forward,
and the considerations to which they have given rise,
the theoretic contention that women can on economic
grounds be treated as improper subjects for the higher
education, intellectual or technical, would, I think, infallibly fall to the ground, but for a difficulty which,
though not universally operative, must still remain
serious as grounded in the nature of things.

I allude to the fact that women who marry usually do so at an early stage of existence, and also that, still more important in this connection, marriage has a quite other bearing on the life of a woman than that which it presents to men. To the latter it means, where its normal conditions are fulfilled, domestic repose, a harbour of refuge from the small worries which more than all else tend to cloud the clear atmosphere of thought and retard intellectual effort. To the former it is the open door to all tedious or tender disquiet. The calls upon the housewife, it is true, may be minimised by a sagely directed system, and the applications of science have in themselves a growing tendency to reduce them; but the claims upon the mother are peremptory, and will remain permanent to the end of time. It is this radical difference in the relation of the sexes to the material facts of existence, which must ever, I think, add another complication to those with which the weaker has to reckon.

It were vain also to close our eyes to the fact that where the means of parents are restricted, and a choice has to be made between girls and boys who have to earn their bread as to which of them shall have the benefit of the higher education, it is the boys in all likelihood who will carry the votes. The possibility of marriage cutting short the expensively provided-for career of the girl will, all other considerations being equal, be alone sufficient to determine her exclusion. And this is a part of the economic problem from which it may frankly be admitted there is no appeal, although its weight will be to some extent balanced by the lesser cost of the college life of girls, and the almost total absence of risk of their involving their parents in debt.

Thus it will be felt that an education completed after the ordinary school term, while it is often pressed upon unwilling boys, is likely to retain for girls the aspect of a privilege of culture, or a luxury in the preparation for daily toil. And not all needy girls, not even a large proportion, are competent to win honourable place in the ranks of the professions for which such advanced education, when specialised, is supposed to fit them. Far must be the desire from any earnest well-wisher of their kind to add to the sum of incapacity which at present encumbers the callings known as intellectual. We want no more doctors without insight, lawyers in whom the only surviving faculty is greed, and teachers without system or sympathy. The dominant sex has already furnished us with too many examples of the harmfulness of misapplied faculty. If our social institutions are such as everywhere to force the square man into the round hole, and *vice versa*, sending the puny children of poverty on foreign service, placing the athlete on the office-stool, and the dunce who has been made a pedant in the pulpit, no advantage could accrue to the world, or, as I think, to the individual, from enlarging the sphere of this anomaly.

There will then remain, when all disabilities not inhering in the nature of things are withdrawn, a large number of women, as there have ever been of men, of the better, no less than of the poorer class, who are incapacitated by nature for the higher forms of activity; whom, in short, no teaching could render intelligent or skilful. These among the sons of gentlemen frequently find an outlet and field for manual labour in the colonies; but what is to become of this army of incompetence, as represented by the daughters to whom this issue is denied?

In our own country, religion offers no material refuge for that multitude of the unmarried, which is yearly increasing. Will any reasonable man or woman maintain that it is an endurable thing that such an army should exist in our midst in a condition of hopeless nullity and almost of starvation?

The letters which besiege the advertiser for a lady-housekeeper or useful companion, are significant of the numerical force of this army, and an interview will rarely fail to reveal the feebleness of the individuals which compose it. Their case is truly pitiful. It is not from the ranks of such that wives are commonly chosen, and it is not a recognised duty in this free country to make provision for unpromising female children.

Among the good things to be desired of the future is the growth of a moral sense better instructed in this particular. No one now doubts that not only the setting aside of entail, but other important changes in testamentary dispositions, are immanent; and it is much to be desired that, seeing the greater perils that beset the path of women, whether gentle or simple, English parents should at last awake to the obligation of making a juster distribution of property between sons and daughters; and where no private means exist, of setting aside some small provision as a dower or a safeguard for the latter.   But that we are slow to learn, we might long since have profited by the example of our nearest neighbours.   There is in France no class above the poorest that does not, often at severe sacrifice, lay aside something for what their customs lead them to regard as the marriage portion of their daughters.   England almost alone enjoys the privilege that all provision for their future can be neglected without entailing reproach upon the authors of their being.

I have now briefly surveyed the ground occupied respectively by the sentimental and the economic aspects of this modern question of women and work; and with the above plea for some added protection to children of the weaker and more burthened sex thrown out by the way, I will close this portion of my subject, and proceed to a more prolonged examination of that point in the controversy, around which the chief forces in opposition have for the moment rallied.

PART III.

*PHYSIOLOGICAL—MEDICAL EVIDENCE AD-
VERSE TO ADVANCED EDUCATION FOR
WOMEN.*

III.

"The mind keeps the body sweet."—Sir Thomas Overbury.

The point in relation of women to work, not, I am fain
to think, of most permanent interest, but of keenest
contention at the present moment, is, then, the physiological, with the deeper and more recondite problem
of the psychological as its inevitable corollary.

The mind of the age, so far as it is concerned in
the question at all, is disturbed by doubts of the effect
which higher intellectual training will exert upon the
bodily health of women, and upon those mental charac-
teristics which, however they may have served as the
targets of masculine wit, have been held, on the whole,
conveniently to prop up that position of male supe-
riority which has been looked on as conducive to the
advantage of the race.

I will not in this place pause to examine, however
briefly, this question on abstract grounds. Whether
it be right or wrong to set a limit to the development
of one half of the body politic, to the end that the other
may triumph at lesser cost, shall at present, as a point
of ethics, form no part of my inquiry. The facts that
I desire here to arrive at are facts of practical expedi-

ency so far as they have up to this present date been substantiated by experiment.

The question thus narrowed resolves itself briefly into this :—In what degree will society gain, in what degree must it be resigned to lose, by the uprising among women which has taken such large proportions in this latter half of the nineteenth century ? How will a movement which, for the sake of the argument, we will suppose it possible to suppress, affect the development of the race physically, morally, and intellectually ? In a word, will it, if encouraged to go forward, be the beginning of a new departure of orderly progress, or an inlet of social anarchy and confusion through the subversion of natural law ?

These are the questions, looked on in relation to humanity as a whole, upon which I have set myself the task of directing such a measure of light as has been gathered up to the present date. For the full and complete answer to propositions involving adjustments of peculiar intricacy, we must be content to wait and watch the gradual development of time. In the meanwhile, with whatever belief in that " soul of good which exists in things evil " I may have set out, I must own to considerable surprise at the amount of definite fact, and the sum of responsible opinion of a reassuring nature, that I have been able to collect within the short time during which I have been qualifying myself for this inquiry. The various authorities to whom I have applied for information, physiologists and educationists—among the latter, directors as well as mistresses of schools and colleges—have not only furnished me with an array of valuable facts, but have expressed their hopeful confidence in the results of female culture with the less reservation as their experience has been the wider. Although I do not seek to disguise the side on which my own sympathies lean, it is no part of my object to make these pages a plea for one side or the other of the case under examination, but rather a candid if slight review of what may fairly be urged on either. It will therefore be well in this place, at the risk of appearing tedious to those who are well abreast of the argument as it now stands, to allow a few of the latest and most authoritative of the witnesses adverse to the movement of female development on the new lines, to recapitulate their testimony in their own terms. That such adverse witness has been making itself heard with some persistency of late will be vaguely known to almost all who turn these pages. I believe it will be in the interests of truth, if not to the advantage of the cause, that to those only partially informed the head and front of the accusations against female culture should be made clear. I can, of course, within the limits I have prescribed myself, make no pretension to an exhaustive, or even fully summarised statement of all that has been urged, and ably urged, against it; but I can confidently claim to have selected from the evidence adverse to the case, that which I have deemed most typical, and never in any instance to have rejected testimony because it appeared damaging to the side on which I believe the path of human progress will ultimately be seen to lie.

The recent campaign, rather let us say the recent skirmish, led by the opponents of advanced education for women, was ushered in at the British Medical Association last autumn by Dr. Withers Moore; and in view of the occasion, and taking into consideration the audience, largely composed of medical men, to which he addressed himself, I think that, in dealing with this psychological section of my subject, I can hardly do better for the less well-informed of my readers than re-state the case for the prosecution as he presented it. From his professional position and the arena in which he chose to be heard, it goes without saying that it would be likely in his hands to present its strongest front. If some of the witnesses called into court on this occasion have been dragged from the long peace of the grave, and made to furnish testimony which bears very imperfectly upon a cause which has been ever since their time in a condition of active flux, the blame of putting forward such ghostly witness is not mine. Sir Benjamin Brodie's name has been held by Dr. Withers Moore a good one to conjure with, and he has made it to figure at the head of his list. Dr. Withers Moore is a doughty champion of the hour, and if some of his band are shadows, we may suppose that he has seen good reason for enlisting them; the

obvious one being, that among living men the choice
of eminent names willing to commit themselves to an
adverse conclusion, is limited.

The deposition of Sir Benjamin Brodie, as adduced
by Dr. Moore, is short, but bearing in mind the degree
of culture enjoyed by the girls of his day (the elderly
women of ours), it is curious :—

"The mind, in the case of girls of the affluent classes, is
educated at the expense of the physical structure, they
spending more time in actual (!) study than their brothers."

It is in this light that the dealings with time in
"Ladies' Schools," stigmatised in the Schools' Inquiry
Commission as ludicrously inadequate, appeared to the
philosopher of thirty years ago.

The next medical authority brought up to furnish
evidence is (again *the late*) Dr. Thorburn of Owen's
College, U.S.   After conceding the urgency of the
struggle for existence which had driven a certain number of gifted women to ignore with safety the physiological difficulties of the majority, Dr. Thorburn goes
on to say :—

" Unfortunately, however, up to this time, no means
have been found which will reconcile this with the
physiological necessity for intermittent work by one
sex.   It becomes, therefore, the duty of every honest
physician to make no secret of the mischief which must
inevitably accrue, not only to many of our young women,
but to our whole population, if the distinction of sex be
disregarded."

E

Once more a medical opinion is quoted on this particular trial of the case, and once more it is *the late* Dr.
E. H. Clarke of the United States who affirms :—

" It is not asserted that all the female graduates of
our schools and colleges are pathological specimens, but
it is asserted that the number of those graduates who
have been disabled, in a greater or less degree, by these
causes is so great as to exite the greatest alarm, and
to demand the most serious attention of the community.
If these causes should continue for the next half-cen-
tury, and increase in the same ratio as they have for
the last fifty years, it requires no prophet to tell that
the women who are to be mothers in our Republic
must be drawn from Transatlantic homes."

Another physician, also from the New World, gives
evidence as follows :—

" I hold that it is not practicable to educate a girl
by the methods found best for a boy without entailing
serious consequences."

And again another, by name Dr. Goodall :—

" From the age of eight to that of sixteen our daughters spend most of their time in the unwholesome atmosphere of the class-room, or in poring over their
books when they should be at play. . . . As the result,
the chief skill of our milliners seems to be directed
towards concealing the lack of organs needful alike to
beauty and to maternity, and the girl of to-day becomes
the barren wife or invalid mother of to-morrow."

Dr. Tuckmann of Cleveland, U.S. (it will be observed

that the voices made to speak in this case, when they do not come to us from the other world, come from the New), relates that in 1881, "Of 800 pupils in a particular high school, nearly 25 per cent. of the girls and 18 per cent. of the boys, from one cause or another, had withdrawn; and that it was found on investigation that of the girls so withdrawn 75 per cent. had left wholly or in part on account of ill-health. Here it appeared that, whether from necessity or from choice, the girls studied more hours out of school than the boys did."

One excerpt from the *Lancet* closes the medical testimony put forward by Dr. Withers Moore; and I give it from a sense of its truth and point in relation to education generally, rather than from any special reference to that of girls, although in the conduct of the latter its lesson may likely enough be more largely applicable. It is as follows:—

" At no epoch of life is the necessity for maintaining the balance between construction and destruction of nervous energy greater than in the period immediately preceding adolescence; and it is just at this time that keen competition is most severely felt in subjecting, as Dr. Ross remarks, the latest evolved portion of the nervous system to a strain so great that only those possessing the best-balanced and strongest system can escape unscathed."

That is the last medical witness brought forward on this particular day of trial which I have taken as typical, if we except some opinions, claiming to be no more than speculative, advanced by Dr. Withers Moore himself. Before subjecting the evidence above given to further examination, it will be but fair to lay before the reader not fully informed of the latest aspect of the charge against female culture, the views, not only of the chairman of the last August meeting of the British Medical Association, but those of so high an authority as Mr. Herbert Spencer. Reserving the opinions put forward under so imposing a name to the last, I will first give the reasons of Dr. Withers Moore for his belief that the higher education of women would be injurious to humankind :—

" I think that it is not good for the human race, considered as progressive, that women should be freed from the restraints which law and custom have imposed upon them, and should receive an education intended to prepare them for the exercise of brain power in competition with men. And I think this because I am persuaded that neither the preliminary training for such competitive work, nor the subsequent practice of it in the actual strife and struggle for existence, can fail to have upon women the effect more or less (and rather more than less) of indisposing them towards and incapacitating them from their own proper function—for performing the part, I mean, which (as the issue of the original differentiation of the sexes) nature has assigned to them in the maintenance and progressive improvement of the human race. This ' higher education ' will hinder those who would have been the best mothers from being mothers at all, or, if it does not hinder them, more or less it will spoil them. And no training will enable themselves to do what their sons might have done."

Dr. Moore, after thus begging the question, proceeds to cite authorities in support of his argument. "A man's fate," he says, quoting an Oxford tutor looking back upon his college experience, "a man's fate all depends upon the nursing—on the mother, not on the father. The father has commonly little to do with the boy till the bent is given and the foundation of character laid. All depends on the mother."

" Galton, in his ' Hereditary Genius,' " continues Dr. Moore, still quoting, "after citing as examples of remarkable women the mothers of Bacon, Buffon, Condorcet, Cuvier, D'Alembert, Gregory, Watts, and others, adds : ' It appears, therefore, to be very important to success in science that a man should have an able mother. Of two men of equal abilities, the one who has a truth-loving mother would be more likely to follow the career of science."

I give the last excerpt because the counsel adverse to progress in female education, has seen fit to give it, although I think it will appear to most unprejudiced persons that it tells distinctly on the other side. We will now hear what Mr. Herbert Spencer has contributed to this discussion in his " Principles of Biology." After noticing that too much bodily labour probably renders women less prolific, he proceeds as follows :—

"That absolute or relative infertility is generally
produced in women by mental labour carried to excess
is more clearly shown. Though the regimen of upper-
class girls is not what it should be, yet, considering
that their feeding is better than that of girls belong-
ing to the poorer classes, while in most respects their
physical treatment is not worse, the deficiency of reproductive power among them may be reasonably attributed
to the overtaxing of their brains, an overtaxing which
produces a serious reaction on the physique. The
diminution of reproductive power is not shown only
by the greater frequency of absolute sterility, nor is it
shown only in the earlier cessation of child-bearing,
but it is also shown in the very frequent inability of
such women to suckle their infants. In its full sense
the reproductive power means the power to bear a well-
developed infant, and to supply that infant with the
natural food for the natural period. Most of the flat-
chested girls who survive their high-pressure education
are unable to do this. Were their fertility measured
by the number of children they could rear without
artificial aid, they would prove relatively very infertile."

With this we will close the case for the complaint;
asking only, before bringing forward the witnesses to
the defence, to be permitted a brief examination of
the foregoing evidence while it is fresh in the mind of
the reader.

And first in order, since we are meant to take it
seriously, we can only say in regard to Sir Benjamin

Brodie's pathetic plea for the overtaxed girls of the affluent classes, that seeing he makes no allusion to the still more hardly used girls who are now being fitted for intellectual callings, he must be assumed, from this omission, to have uttered his warning so long ago that it utterly fails to reach the case on its present advanced lines. If time, as he says, were unduly taxed to furnish the intellectual outfit of the pupils of " Ladies' Seminaries " in the last generation, it was squandered on what were then known as " accomplishments "—a smattering of music and drawing, something less than a smattering of modern languages, and for all of natural science " the use of the globes." Now it is plain that unless women are to cease to be the companions of men, and are to be maintained systematically at some lower animal level, they must share their progress in culture even when directed to no utilitarian end, as, according to the law of development, they will share their increasing aptitudes. In the history of the race the obstinate favour with which practices tending to disqualify women from their due share in the world's advance is regarded as no new thing. The imprisonment of women in harems and the mutilation of the Chinese woman's foot are potent examples, and are sufficient in themselves to point the lesson that no wrong can be done to the part, that will not revenge itself upon the whole. A stagnant element in the midst of a growing body is a centre of disease and death.

Next to that of Sir B. Brodie's we have heard the

testimony of Dr. Thorburn, who fairly takes count of
the keenness of the contest in which women are now
largely engaged, and admits that certain of them are
capable of bearing their part in it without suffering.
The caution to the greater number with which he
follows up this admission implies no more than the
recognition of a fact which none may dispute, viz.,
that in the race of life women are, to an appreciable
degree, weighted by the conditions of sex. As a warning against over-strained, and thus fruitless and harmful endeavour, these words of Dr. Thorburn are worthy
of as much consideration as the exigencies of the case
will permit. As discouragement to already burthened
if necessary effort, they have the hollow mocking sound
of all utterance resulting from imperfect sympathy.

The reproach wherewith Dr. E. H. Clarke charges
the mental culture and activity of his female compatriots is a serious and more definite indictment.
That according to him a considerable number of the
graduates of female colleges and schools should be
" pathological specimens " is an alleged fact that can
hardly be accepted without careful examination. Dr.
Clarke, like most of those who have been made to
speak on this occasion, dates from the United States,
in which many feverish elements, unknown or less
known to ourselves, are seething. The question, everywhere sufficiently complicated, presents itself in the
New World entangled with even more considerations
alien to the result, and tending to confuse the judg-

ment. The climate of the great Western continent has been found extremely exhausting by its not yet fully Americanised inhabitants; and the life of a young ambitious people, bent on distancing all creation, is too rapid of itself, apart from systematised mental exercise, not frequently to cause undue strain on the nervous energies. But with all allowance made for the difference of the environment, I am withheld by a quite overwhelming amount of counter-testimony from accepting the conclusions of the learned doctor. I happen to have in my hands a book published in New York, "The Education of American Girls," in which every college and high school of note in the States, up to the year 1871, has contributed its quota of information, and, in many cases, of statistics. While duly acknowledging the need of care in bringing into play faculties which, having been discountenanced in the sex from the beginning of time, have no hereditary tendency to activity, the sum of evidence brought into the inquiry by the experienced educationists who have combined in this work is such as to cause every impartial opponent, basing his antagonism on physiological grounds, to reconsider, if not altogether to withdraw from, his position. To proceed.

After Dr. Clarke, Dr. Emmett is brought forward to utter what in effect is a mere personal opinion, to wit, that it is not practicable to educate a girl by the methods found good for a boy without entailing undesirable consequences. Into this matter of detail we

need not enter here. The question is, not how shall
women be educated? but shall they be educated at all?
It is probably inevitable, at the present stage of the
experiment, that the course and manner of study which
obtains for men should be the gauge of efficiency for
the education of women. In the future, when experience has affirmed the particular developments for
which female faculty is best fitted—the lines by following which it will bring the most serviceable contribution
to the common store—we may expect to hear less of
this rivalry. It would probably be no loss if in the
end it were found desirable that the education of women
should be advanced on somewhat different methods.

When we hear from Dr. Goodall, who is the next
witness with whom we have had to deal, that most of
the time of growing girls is spent in "unwholesome" air,
there would seem little need for farther inquiry into
the causes of the physical deterioration he laments as
having come under his notice. Bad air, whether of
the class-room or elsewhere, but more especially of the
class-room, where much is taken in by the mind and
little given off by the system, would of itself be sufficient to vitiate a testimony to the evil effects of
learning upon health, even if far more broadly and
securely based than in the face of counter-evidence we
can allow this to be.

The experience of Dr. Tuckmann would seem to
have been indeed disastrous. It relates to a " particular high school," but he does not himself par-

ticularise so far as to give us its name. It is manifestly not one of those which have furnished statistical
information to the book to which I have alluded.
It is, as we gather, a school of mixed boys and girls.
That the boys should have suffered in health to the
extent of 18 per cent., against the " nearly 25 per
cent." of the girls, is in some degree reassuring to
those whose duty it is to apply this serious example
to the case of the latter. The conditions of study
and the whole environment must have been very prejudicial to health for so large a percentage of boys to
have succumbed to them. That the more sensitive
organisation of the girls should have exposed them as
readier victims was what might reasonably have been
expected ; more especially as we are told that, in spite
of their frail health, they were suffered to study more
hours out of school than the boys. The evidence of
this witness must, I think, be taken with grave reservation.

The remarks culled from the *Lancet* are worthy
of the respectful consideration which their subject
is in fact receiving from the many able men and
women who are devoting themselves to the theory
and practice of education. Far be it from me to
make light of the danger therein pointed out, or to
take so much as a feather's weight from the warning
as applied to the sex, which being the more im-
pressible, is most easily stimulated to harmful effort.
Without assuming a congenital deficiency which facts,

to say the least, have put in doubt, the caution must
be admitted as more needed in the case of girls than
of boys; but I think it will also appear in the course
of this inquiry, that to this characteristic the educators
of the former need no awakening.

From the above examination of medical statements
we turn and close with the generalisations made from
the more purely philosophic standpoint. And here we
encounter Dr. Withers Moore's opinion, that it is not
good for the human race that women should be freed
from the restraints of law and custom, or be "prepared
for the exercise of brain-power in competition with
men." He gave it as the ground of this opinion, that
the training for and subsequent practice of such competitive work in the strife and struggle for existence
would tend to indispose and incapacitate them from
the bearing of children.

Now, since it is clear that of women who must
labour for the bread they eat, duties to the race notwithstanding, a proportion, probably larger than that
of men, are incapable of working effectively with their
hands, it follows that, if they are not to starve or be
thrown upon the streets, they must labour in some sort
with their heads. This position will be seen to be
undeniable. Dr. Moore's proposition then reduces itself
to this: that a large number of women may and
must work, only they must do so without adequate
training; in his own words, they should not "receive
an education intended to prepare them for the exercise

of brain-power in competition with men." They are
thus to be kept in the position of quacks and
charlatans, or of the rabble following the regular
army of qualified labour. The "strife and struggle
for existence" (I again quote) are not ignored by this
speculative philosopher, only the battle of life, when
fought by women, must be fought in fetters. I will
refrain here from remark upon the end for which the
bye-laws which press so cruelly upon one sex are to
be kept up, since I shall have to dwell upon it at
greater length farther on; but what, it must be asked
before dismissing the views of Dr. Moore, can have
induced him to impart in this connection the experience of an Oxford tutor, when he says that "a
man's fate depends all upon his mother's nursing,
the father having little to do with the boy till the
foundation of character is laid"? Can it be that the
physiologist underlying the philosopher sees in the
word "nursing" only the exercise of a function in
which the human female shows to considerable disadvantage in comparison with other mammals, or that
he believes the foundation of character to be wholly
dependent on the quality of a man's first food?
Farther on, one is tempted again to ask if this
physical ministration is the sole meaning he affixes to
the words of Mr. Galton: "It is important to success
in science that a man should have an *able* mother"?
Only here the supposition receives a check, since it is
stated that this mother should be also "truth-loving;"

and in this respect the connection between food and
faculty must be acknowledged even by Dr. Moore to
fail. The "truth-loving mother," so desirable a factor in
the production of a man of science, can be no other
than one who has an impassioned sense of the value of
truth for its own sake. Now if there is one thing
above all else calculated to maintain the rarity of such
an apparition, it is that feint, that pretence of education, that training merely to please, which has through
all the centuries been the acknowledged aim of female
teaching. Thus the examples of eminent men having
had able mothers, which have been invited to do service in the cause against the sound education of the
sex, must, I think, be acknowledged as highly damaging to their employers.

Among the speculators who gave their views on the
occasion of the Brighton Congress, not the least worthy
of attention was Mr. Lawson Tait. After declaring
himself an advocate of women's rights, he went on to
affirm that " exceptional culture would infallibly have
the tendency to remove the fittest individuals, those
most likely to add to the production of children of
high-class brain-power, from out of the ranks of
motherhood." It does not appear exactly in what
manner the "exceptional culture" of these well-endowed
individuals would work to their exclusion from this
category. We are left in doubt as to whether their
minds would be ruined by over-exercise, or their
inclinations turned aside from that which, if not the

whole, is by many regarded as the chief duty of woman. In either case, the danger, if certified, would be serious. That the woman of cultivated intellect must transmit a heritage of ineptitude to her offspring is a grave charge, one which we decline to accept without evidence more circumstantial than it has ever yet been attempted to bring forward. We have a right to throw upon the accusing side the onus of proof that the children of highly cultivated mothers show a larger proportion of the imbecile and incapable, if not wholly idiotic, than those of the comparatively uneducated, before giving in to this worst of all the scares which beset the path of female progress. The limited experience which thus far could be shown in this matter might be found to point to a far different conclusion. So awful a contingency would indeed be a burthen to load on the motherly heart which exists *in posse* in most women and girls, and every shred of testimony calculated to throw light on the subject would be gratefully welcomed by every honest inquirer. In the meanwhile, in the present dearth or paucity of verified fact, it is permitted to the woman to hope that the results of intellectual discipline will, in her case, as in that of her partner, be handed on, to the manifest increase of the inheritance of the race.

On the assumption that more systematised mental activity may have a tendency to substitute, and this chiefly among girls the most highly gifted, other interests in place of those for which the sex is by

many supposed to exist, I will not now dwell, as I
shall have to return to it hereafter.   The gain of
freedom has generally been found more than the loss,
and may, must, be trusted to do so in a case involving
adjustments of such obscurity and delicacy as would
seem to forbid the clumsy interference of ill-informed
agents from without.

I will now pass on to an examination of those
propositions of Mr. Herbert Spencer, which, in view of
the importance which attaches to his authority, I have,
in venturing to question, reserved to the last.   The
conclusion to which his remarks, as given in his
"Principles of Biology," tend, is the same precisely as
that aimed at in the speculations of Dr. Moore.   The
words of the poet, in which Nature is charged with
being careful of the type while careless of the individual life, might serve as motto and justification to
the views of the philosopher.   It is clear that the
preservation by multiplication of the type takes precedence in his mind of the perfecting, still more of
the happiness, of the individual; and further, that in
his view, however it may be with the individual man,
the individual woman can in no case be an end in
herself, but must be content to exist for the purpose
of giving birth to a being in whose hands, to say the
least, the progress of humanity has been slow, and
the less satisfactory in those times and at those
places where he has had it most wholly to himself.
The difference of the view I desire to advance in

opposition to this of Mr. Spencer is fundamental. I maintain that facts which are every day accumulating forbid us to accept the inherently feeble and non-evolutionary character of the female intellect implied in all restrictions, as an established conclusion. The area which includes the things that "women cannot do," is being trenched upon from day to day; insomuch that a suspicion forces itself upon all but the inveterately prejudiced, that the circle which has been drawn round their power of attainment is no better than a circle of chalk. If this be so, then both halves of the family of man are alike sharers of those infinite, purely human possibilities, of which nature offers only the starting-point; and the attempt to regulate the whole life of a being so endowed, with reference solely, or even chiefly, to a single animal function, must be characterised as in the highest degree invidious.

But apart from the assumption that woman is no other than a channel through which the higher gifts and endowments of the race may pass but can never inhere, we may find in those opinions of our great sociologist which we have quoted, another equally questionable proposition. If I read him aright, Mr. Herbert Spencer accepts it as proven that a high degree of reproductive power is the best gauge of physical well-being. I humbly submit that this is a conclusion which recently observed facts have done something more than put in doubt. The census returns are eloquent in refutation of this fallacy. From

F

them we may learn that the increase of the population is never greater than in times of sharp distress from scarcity of food and work. The number of children born in the poor purlieus of great towns, and in those Irish cabins where want and laziness combine to reduce existence to the lowest level compatible with its continuance, has long been matter for curious remark; and the history of famine, to which so many terrible chapters have been added from life in the wide field of our Indian possessions, brings its quota of evidence to the same effect, viz., that the human race at no time shows so great a tendency to numerical increase as when it exists just short of starvation-point. It is no part of my business to account for the fact here stated—a fact which every one who chooses may verify for himself. The horticulturist will know that the law thus controlling reproduction in the animal kingdom has its counterpart in the vegetable. It is not the most flourishing plant, the tree living and seemingly exulting in life on its own account, that breaks forth into fullest flower and bears the largest quantity of fruit. Gardeners are well aware of the advantage to this end of keeping the "subject" pot-bound, or otherwise curtailed of expansive power employed for its own benefit. The possession of vital force is in every organised being restricted within variable measure, and thus its exceptional activity at any given point must mean a corresponding withdrawal either equally from the entire sum, or specially from some one function. Such being the case, it would seem that equality in the distribution of force would be a sounder end at which to aim, a better gauge of the health of the individual, than a high degree of power to increase its kind.

We hear, on the authority of Mr. Herbert Spencer, that "too much bodily labour renders women less prolific." Precisely; such a result was to be expected on the principle laid down. We are told also that comparative infecundity is even more generally the effect of "mental labour carried to excess." That also follows naturally from the premises, if our facts, as stated, are correct. I should go a step farther, and suggest that such comparative infecundity might be expected to accrue to either sex as the result of mental exertion, albeit falling far short of what could reasonably be termed excessive. The paucity of descendants of men of genius may be held to give colour to this view. Altogether, as species and genera rise in dignity, their reproductive power becomes less; and the same tendency in a minor degree may be remarked in individuals, more especially in those of the human family. We may take Mr. Herbert Spencer's statement as sufficiently proved, that the better-fed and better-taught women of the affluent classes are, relatively to the suffering poor, infertile; but when we are asked to conclude from this fact that owing to the modicum of teaching of which they are usually the subjects, they experience loss to physical well-being for which no care or feeding will atone, we are forced to emphatically withhold our assent.

Let us for a moment imagine ourselves laying hands

on any score of women, taken in the flower of their age from Mr. Herbert Spencer's "infertile higher classes," and confronting them with an equal number of their ill-fed contemporaries from our slums and rookeries, those who give proof of their abundant power to recruit our overflowing population. Will the boldest opponent of female culture venture to affirm that the latter would carry the day in any competition where health and beauty, physical well-being, and enjoyment of life were in the balance? I am persuaded that not Mr. Spencer himself would expect confirmation of his theory from such a test. So much for that condition of the mothers, or future mothers, which is conducive to the greatest numerical increase. If we should proceed—Mr. Lawson Tait notwithstanding—from a comparison of the physical and mental state of the two classes of women to a comparison of the quality of their respective offspring, we have no need to ask assistance of imagination in setting them face to face for judgment. It is with long-established tabulated facts that we have here to deal; the death-rate of the infants of the working poor being only too eloquent on this head. After large allowance made for the other evil conditions incident to infant life in this class, it will still appear that for little ones drawing sustenance from mothers who, according to Mr. Herbert Spencer, are so much better able to furnish it than their educated sisters, an appalling proportion succumbs and is carried to the grave before the age at which they are weaned. The loss of child-life in the prolific class of the very poor before the age of five years, is a thing to make the heart ache when we reflect on what is implied in it : the low condition of that physical being which is the primary source of infant joy, and the sorrow, not to speak of the lost labour, of the women who have given these children birth. It is, however, only the physical question that immediately concerns the argument. The children drawing nourishment from the mothers who are held up as examples of maternal efficiency, are seen to die in larger numbers than could readily be accounted for at this comparatively sheltered period of their existence, if the constitutions they inherited were not relatively feeble.

I have taken the "upper classes" generally for comparison, as presented by Mr. Herbert Spencer. If I have been guilty of some unfairness in making his "poorer class" the *very poor*, I have been drawn into it by his insistence on fertility as a supreme guarantee of health. This has naturally induced me to seek it where it was most to be found. That Mr. Herbert Spencer has seen fit to take "upper-class girls" generally as instances of the effects of mental over-strain on fertility, is a point in the contention which rather tends to strengthen the view of that natural modification of the reproductive power which announces itself as the result of an equable human development. The ordinary level of education among "upper-class girls" may even yet be taken to be as low as is consistent with the maintenance of health in beings with busy brains, and no work to do but of their own making; and so much has been conceded to female progress by public opinion, so much in the matter of advanced education is an accomplished fact, that from this very moderate degree of culture, the combined arguments of the wisest of speculative philosophers would hardly induce the age to recede.

How much farther the real work of the brain, in which a considerable contingent of young women are at this time engaged, will go in exemplifying the operation of a law which will present itself to many persons as the possible solution of a social difficulty looming in the not very remote future, it is not for us at present to decide; the experiment is too young to have furnished all the data needful to a definite conclusion. At this point it would be perhaps wise to limit our view for the moment to the effect of advanced culture on the individual woman—her health, her happiness, and her usefulness in her human sphere, not forgetting that driving force of circumstances which has so much to do in urging her forward on the new path of her intellectual progress and more systematised effort.

With this examination of Mr. Herbert Spencer's opinions of the probable effect of the more liberal culture now within the reach of women, upon the race, I will conclude the case, of which I have endeavoured to give a fair presentment from the adverse side, and proceed to array such counter-evidence as, with limited opportunity, I have been able to collect in the course of an inquiry whose primary object was personal enlightenment.

PART IV.

MEDICAL TESTIMONY AND STATISTICAL EVIDENCE FAVOURABLE TO THE ADVANCED EDUCATION OF WOMEN.

IV.

A CONSIDERABLE amount of purely medical testimony to the supposed evil effect upon health of the higher culture of women has been duly set forth in the beginning of the physiological section of this inquiry. It is now my part to confront this adverse testimony with that elicited on the other side, and to show that even in a profession where a tendency to regard the human subject chiefly from the physical point of view must naturally exist, and where also the female student commonly presents herself only for treatment in sickness, the strength of the countervailing evidence is such as abundantly to reassure the doubting friends of progressive education, and to set the more candid of its adversaries to a more cautious striking of the balance.

As time is so important a factor in a question which, like this with which we are dealing, is in a state of continuous if gradual flux, I will begin the case for what may be called the defence, by first citing from the authorities which have generously lent their aid to this inquiry, those of distinguished practitioners whose experience brings them fully abreast of the movement in its latest development.

To Sir William Gull the endeavour of women after sounder intellectual training owes the following succinct and profound expression of sympathy. There is no need to dwell upon the width of the experience of which it is the outcome. An opinion so unambiguous and so ably maintained, issuing from such a quarter, will give food for thought to all but the most inveterately prejudiced, and is well calculated to clear the air for young female students, of those doubts and fears which alarmists have been busy in creating.

In accordance with his expressed desire, I quote Sir William Gull's own words from the MS. before me—

"In the light of medical experience, the advantage to health of good and even high intellectual training for girls and young women cannot be doubted.

"After due attention to the ordinary requirements of physical health in respect of food, air, exercise, and sleep, nothing more essentially contributes to physical development and good health than the education of the senses and the mental faculties.

"Without this object the mind is left listless, and the bodily functions in consequence are apt to become languid; so that constantly the physician is consulted for a weak state which more mental energy would correct.

"If it be true, as experience shows it is, that over-mental tension seriously weakens and exhausts, it is equally true that for every such instance, at least in the well-to-do classes of the community, there are many more where life is but a burden, in consequence of the mind having no aim or object before it to call forth and quicken its operation. So that on all grounds the intellectual training of women should be advanced as far as the faculties and other circumstances of each individual will admit of it.

"The mind has its gymnastics as the body has, and both should be limited within the individual's natural power. If this be so managed, the exercises of body and mind will increase this power without danger of injury or strain, and with no result but what is good. The powers and endurance of the body are, all other things being equal, advanced by moral and intellectual training—if only in this, that they supply rules for avoiding excess or defect, and give direction and proportion to the energies.

"Hence an educated woman is on a higher physiological level of capacity in relation to all her duties.

"We may therefore believe that it is no longer a question whether women should be highly educated or not, but rather what constitutes the best and highest intellectual training, which must of course vary according to the circumstances of individuals ; and further, with what stores should the mind be furnished, beyond such as the exercises of training supply.

"If it should be thought, as some seem to have thought, that the only office of women is 'to marry, bear children, guide the house,' this would, I have no doubt, be better intrusted to a highly intellectually trained woman, than to one left to the common accidents of events—to the bookstall and the piano. That in the harder competitions of life women may, on the mere ground of want of endurance, fail in comparison with men, will be admitted ; but it is no ground for their exclusion from the best lines of study and the most improved methods of teaching.

(Signed)   WILLIAM N. GULL."

My next witness on this side of the contention will be Dr. Lionel Beale, his testimony being an exerpt from a letter dated also the 15th of last December, and addressed to the remarkable woman at the head of Cheltenham College, to whose efforts the cause of female culture is deeply indebted.   Dr. Beale writes as follows :—

" Should I be in Cheltenham again, I will certainly try to arrange a call.   I should be interested to see healthy girls who have not suffered from 'over-pressure,' of which condition I have never yet beheld a real case, while the sufferers from want of exercise of their faculties are legion.   Of course, stupid young people ought not to be worked like those of average or superior mental power ; but that seems to be all. As for keeping nine down in order that one may not be ' over-pressed,' it is absurd.

" Looking at the British brain in general, I think one would say there is even now much more prospect of de-generation from want of use than damage from over-pressure.   (Signed)   LIONEL E. BEALE.

" *December* 1886."

The statement I am permitted to cite from a letter

of Dr. Herman Weber, in response to my inquiries, records a somewhat different experience, and altogether sounds a less confident note ; but apart from the need of care in the conduct of study, which no experienced and thoughtful educationist would deny, Dr. Weber's conclusions will be seen not greatly to differ from those just cited.

"Now and then," writes Dr. Weber, "I have met in my professional work with girls and young women who had injured themselves while working at college or at home. In almost every one of these cases, however, the illness was due rather to mistakes committed in studying than to the intellectual efforts *per se.* Such mistakes, for instance, were want of sufficient air and exercise ; injudicious arrangements as to meals and sleep ; imperfect ventilation of bed-rooms and sitting-rooms ; over-anxiety about the result of examinations.

"I cannot say that girls who devote themselves to judicious intellectual work, suffer more than those who follow the ordinary pursuits of fashionable society; but young women cannot any more than young men disobey with impunity the commands of hygiene.

(Signed)   HERMANN WEBER.

"*December* 1886."

I will take leave, in pursuance of this part of my subject, to turn from some quite recent authorities still in reserve, to others of older date, which, as touching the question of the effect of study upon general health,

find a more fitting place at this stage of inquiry
than later on, when those effects will be regarded
from the point of view more especially of brain dis-
turbance.

Mr. Solly, F.R.S., formerly surgeon of St. Thomas's
Hospital, contributed the result of his experience to
the Schools Inquiry Commission on the Education of
Girls in the following terms :—

" As an old physiologist, I wish to give my
opinion. I know that the more the brain is exercised, gradually and without undue exertion, the better
that brain will be capable of producing the results
for which it was formed. I am *quite certain* that
there would be less illness amongst the upper classes
if their brains were more regularly and systematically
worked."

Again, referring to the report of the Schools Inquiry
Commission, I find it affirmed by Dr. Brigham, one
of the witnesses called in that investigation :—

" The cultivation of the mind at a proper time of
life is not injurious, but beneficial. If the functions
of the brain are not exercised, it diminishes in size.
When any organ diminishes for want of proper exercise,
the whole system sympathises, and thus the health
becomes impaired. From this view of the subject I
cannot doubt but that *the exercise of the intellect tends
to procure and to perpetuate sound health.*"

Dr. Aldis, in the same report, is recorded to have
said :—

" *I am perfectly convinced* as the result of many years' practice, that whatever tends to develop the minds of women will have the best effect on their moral and physical as well as intellectual health."

Not to exhaust the attention of the reader by repetition of the same general view stated in different terms, I will conclude by selecting from the considerable amount of purely medical evidence which still lies before me on this side of the case, the witness only of two specialists, men whose lives have been devoted to the study of brain-disease, and whose testimony upon the subject under consideration must therefore be regarded as of peculiar value. The three opinions last cited bear the date of the Girls' Schools Inquiry Commission, 1867; those which are now to be produced are, like the evidence of Sir W. Gull, Dr. Hermann Weber, and Dr. Beale, of as recent date as December of last year; in one case still later. Dr. Needham of Barnland Asylum, near Gloucester, states :—

" I have no kind of hesitation in saying in this letter, what I have already expressed to you, and for many years have been convinced of, that although there is no doubt such a thing as over-pressure, which may lead to disease by the undue and unrelaxing strain upon limited mental and physical powers, a much more fertile source of disease exists in our class and that above ours in the absence of an aim in life worthy of the name, and in the indolence, self-indulgence, and unhealthy emotionalism which are the results. Women

never could have been intended to be the useless creatures so many of them are."

The name of Dr. Langdon Downe will be felt to be
in the highest degree authoritative in this connection.
At the opening of the present year I received from him
the full expression of opinion which I herewith lay
before the reader :—

"There is one subject of great interest at the present
time, which is made the topic of addresses from presi-
dential chairs as well as of numerous articles in periodi-
cal literature : I mean the higher education of women.

"The doctrine which has been promulgated of late is,
that the proper culture of the faculties of women will
make them less capable of becoming mothers of men.
There has been hitherto no objection to their being
taught everything relating to art, music, or their emotional life, but directly there are attempts made to cultivate their judgment, to teach them how to reason, and
to inculcate habits of self-control, we are met by clamours
which, in my opinion, are not based on experience, and,
so far as the ætiology of feeble-mindedness is concerned,
are likely to be prejudicial.

"If there is anything more certain than another
about the production of idiocy, it is the danger which
arises from the culture of one side only of a woman's
nature. So long as human mothers are trained only on
their emotional side, responsive to the least unexpected
sound, unreasoning as to the world of nature about them,
and thrown into emotional paroxysm by the sights and
trials which will be sure to cross their path, they will,

from my point of view, be the more likely to become the mothers of idiots. Without advocating over-pressure, which is as bad for the neurotic boy as for the neurotic girl, and which is to be avoided during the developmental life of the one as well as during the developmental life of the other, there can be no reason why the faculties which it is now known they possess should not be cultivated, so as to make them not only fit to be mothers of men, but also companions and helpers of men. At all events, let the trial be made without prejudice, and let us welcome the advent of a time when women shall not be merely the frivolous toys of an hour, but have and enjoy the privileges and rights of which it is absurd to deprive them.

" My statistics show that we must look mainly to the health and mental life of the parents. They point to the importance of training our sons to be temperate and our daughters to be self-possessed. They indicate that we should seek alliances for the latter with men from a healthy stock; that our sons should avoid as wives those whose emotions are cultivated at the sacrifice of their judgment and self-control. They show that idiocy is often the outcome of a gradual process, in which the race becomes more and more degenerate, requiring only an insignificant factor to produce the direst results.

(Signed)   LANGDON DOWNE."

With these important statements I close the direct medical testimony to the advantage of a sound education, judiciously carried out, upon the health of that half of the race which, under the received title of the "weaker," has up to very recent years been excluded from

G

processes which for the male mind have been held to be
strengthening. It can hardly be necessary to recall to
the remembrance of those seriously interested in this
inquiry the opinions favourable to advanced female
culture pronounced by Sir Spencer Wells at the opening
of the Sanitary Congress, or those which have been often
made public by Mrs. Garret Anderson and other eminent
physiologists, to the effect that the restless vacuity of
mind still largely prevailing among girls of the affluent
classes, is a more insidious enemy to health than the
over-pressure of which so much has been said, even where
it exists. I may, however, be allowed to add to this
direct medical testimony, while dealing with the physiological portion of my work, an excerpt from a lecture
delivered at the Royal Institution on " Man's Power
over Himself to Prevent or Control Insanity : "—

" As, when matter has become organised, if the
process of change occasioned by the vital force be impeded or arrested, the plant pines away and perishes ;
as, after the organs of locomotion have been superadded,
the animal debarred from the use of them languishes
and becomes diseased; so man, if he give not full
scope to the intellectual force, becomes subject to evils
greater than animals can ever know, because his nature
is of higher order.

" Every one who has given rational attention to
the subject has been earnest in recommending application to some study which should occupy the mind
without agitating the feelings, as one of the most

effectual modes of counteracting morbid impressions. The registers of lunatic asylums show the number of female patients to exceed that of males by nearly one-third. We have the assurance of professional men, well experienced in the treatment of the insane, that nothing is more rare than to find among them a person of a judiciously cultivated mind."

It will be seen to how great an extent the facts here stated reinforce those contained in the evidence of Dr. Langdon Downe and Dr. Needham.

Thus far we have been regarding the question of the influence upon the health of women of that higher education which can alone come under the name of " *work* " from the aspect in which it may be supposed chiefly to affect the " race." We may now, however, give a brief glance to its observed effect on the physical development of the woman in her individual capacity.

When we hear vaguely of injury to health produced by a given cause, we are driven, in the absence of definite, well-authenticated information concerning the forms and degree in which impaired health manifests itself, to seek for the more steady light which may be found in the relative duration of lives which have been known as subject to the supposed insalubrious influence.

Although longevity may not be accepted as an absolutely conclusive test of the degree of health enjoyed during life, it must, when coupled with a fair amount of labour accomplished, be allowed to be as good a gauge as any which in our present dearth of information we can come by. The length of days commonly enjoyed by brain-workers is certified to by Dr. Burnand in his " *Hygiène des Gens de Lettres :* "—

"The class of learned men who have lived more than seventy years includes the most distinguished that ever existed. Of 1 5 2 *savans* taken at *hazard,* one half from the Academy of *Belles-Lettres,* the other from that of Sciences of Paris, it was found that the average of life was above sixty-nine years to each man. I conclude that the cultivation of the mind at a proper time of life contributes to produce good health, not only by exercising one of the most important organs of the body, but by placing reason and conscience on the throne."

If it be objected that the above facts refer exclusively to men, and the even greater necessity for placing reason and conscience on the throne with the more emotional half of the human family be not admitted, it may still be seen that, although, for obvious reasons, no induction on so large a scale can yet be made in the case of learned women, such facts as we possess, all point in the direction which parity of reasoning would indicate, viz. : that the same rule applies to either sex, and perhaps more notably to that which is by nature the more impulsive.

Miss Beale, in her preface to the " Report of the Commissioners of Inquiry into the Condition of Girls' Schools," has furnished some interesting facts in this regard :—

" Mathematics," we read, " at least, do not appear
to have an injurious effect upon the health of women "
(judged by longevity).   " Maria Lewen, author of a
book of astronomical tables published in " (what to
women were then dark ages) "the seventeenth century,
lived to past seventy.   Maria Agnesi, the writer of
what we hear, on the authority of Professor De Morgan,
is 'a well-matured treatise on algebra and the differential calculus, inferior to none of its day in knowledge and arrangement,' survived to the age of eighty-
one.   Miss Caroline Herschel, the active assistant of
her brother, and one of the first women-mathematicians
of her day, lived to the age of ninety-seven.   While
the great age of Mrs. Somerville will be a case in point
familar to all."

I have thus far set against the charges of damage
to the health of the individual and the race, coming
from the ranks of the medical profession, only the
countervailing testimony of high and, in several cases,
quite recent medical authority.   Weighty as are the
names of those who have pronounced so unfalteringly
in favour of the effect of a better education than that
heretofore accorded to girls, I should probably have
shortened this portion of my inquiry had an amount
of statistics ranging over a sufficient period been
ready for use.   Such statistic is, however, with us,
still in the making; indeed, so far as I can gather,
scarcely a hand is yet put to the work.   The means

of sound and improved education in colleges, high, middle-class, and Board schools, are within the reach of all, and eagerly seized on by the majority of parents or guardians of the young; but little time or thought has seemingly yet been spared from the active conduct of the movement for any scientific statement of its results upon health. It may be that in this country, any such tabulation would at present be premature. The nearest approach to a body of fact so systematised I owe to the kindness and energy of Miss Beale, who, as the head of one of the oldest establishments for advanced education in England, has had a longer period from which to glean than that generally possessed." * Statistical tables are a dry study in any case, and the space devoted to this portion of my subject has, in the absence of statistics of adequate completeness, been given up to testimony drawn from personal experience.

The American tables which have reached me include a far more extended area in space and time than any which exist for ourselves, and, when viewed in connection with the cries of medical alarmists from the States, samples of which have been duly given in a foregoing page, must be held as something more than significant of what may be reckoned on when our own case comes to be fully made out.

We find in the Report of the Committee of Health

* Since the above was written, Miss Mackillip, Principal of the Ladies' Collegiate School, Londonderry, has also favoured me with some returns, which will be found in the Appendix.

Statistics, published at Boston in May 1885, that the Association of Collegiate Alumni, warned by the charges of over-pressure of the delicate and nervous American girl, which were still rife up to that date, had " bent its energies to the task of discovering upon what actual basis the claims regarding the physical incapacity of college-women rested." A series of forty questions, prepared with the utmost care, was submitted to the alumni of the colleges included in the Association, and answers were received from 705 women, the net results of which I will here only briefly state. But before proceeding to these results, it would be well to direct attention to the fact distinctly set forth, that it was not college education, or advanced education in any form, which first called public attention to the lack of vigour in American women. An article published in *Putnam's Magazine*, before even Vassar (their earliest established woman's college) was founded, makes no mention, in an examination of the causes of the " Little Health of American Women," of excessive mental labour, but indicates other conditions as adequate to the result deplored.

To proceed to a digest of the 705 returns obtained. Against the adjectives, " excellent, good, indifferent, poor," which were suggested as typical conditions of health, we find the following numbers :—

272 report themselves as in " excellent health."

277 as in " good health."

85 as in " indifferent ; " and 35 as in " poor health."

There were 36 others not classing themselves under
any of these heads, whose total answers allowed of their
being averaged under the term "fair."

If we add together those in "excellent" and "good
health," we find they constitute nearly 78 per cent. of
the entire number; while if to this standard be added
those who admitted their health as "fair," we bring
up the ratio to 83 per cent., leaving 17 per cent. to
be placed in the list of the bodily infirm.

But, in mitigation of even this result, the researches
of the Association prove, that "when these same 705
students entered college, 140 of them, or 20 per cent.,
were below the standard of fair health, so that the
college training, instead of adding to, seems to have
detracted from, the number of invalids, and can be
counted as a positive physical benefaction."

This opinion, that education in general, and college
education in particular, is distinctly physically beneficial
to women, has been strengthened by the statistics thus
far collected, and by the general tone of the criticisms
upon the published results, and finds repeated and
emphatic expression in all the later reports on the
subject which have reached me from America.

There is a circumstance of interest, if not directly
bearing upon this portion of the discussion, which may
be noted in passing. The publication of a full catalogue
of the graduates of Vassar College reveals the fact that
comparatively only a small number of the Vassar
students had entered the state of matrimony. The

question is put by Mrs. Annie G. Howes, as chairman
of the Health Committee :—

"Are the causes producing this social phase
permanent or temporary? and further:—Does the
disinclination to marriage lie exclusively with one
sex?"

It is the opinion of Mrs. Howes, that if it can be
shown that the permanent tendency of highly cultured
women is towards celibacy, the advanced system of
education is not likely to become generally popular
beyond the small circle of those who resolve early in
life to devote themselves to professional pursuits.

The average age of the women who responded to
the circular was $28\frac{1}{2}$ years; of that number but 27.8
per cent. were married in 1886. The proportion
given is probably smaller than that actually existing
between married and unmarried students, since it is
manifestly more difficult to obtain the correct addresses
of those who had changed both their name and residence
since leaving college. Thus many of the circulars may
have failed to reach the married graduates. But even
allowing for a gain in percentage as the correct esti-
mate, a report issued in England in 1875, showing
the result that out of 1000 women, 496, very nearly
one half, living between the ages of fifteen and sixty,
were married, would point to the conclusion that college
graduates, in America at least, are not so prone as
other women to enter upon married life.

I state the apparent fact as presented above, but

will not linger here to enter upon a consideration of
its possible cause or causes.   That the fears so often
expressed for the welfare of the children of the future
mothers of America "will be somewhat allayed by the
report given of the family conditions of 1 30 alumni
who have had children," is more germane to this
portion of my study.   "The exceptional record of
good health among these children, and their low death-
rate (I quote from the Report), are strong evidences
that the powers of motherhood have not suffered from
college work."

In conclusion Mrs. Howe remarks :—

" We have every reason to congratulate ourselves
that our willingness to search for the truth, and to
bear the responsibility of its verdict, has led to so
encouraging and satisfactory a revelation.   We can
feel confident that a higher education for women is
in harmony with that vast law of the survival of the
fittest which guides the activities of the dim future."

With these words I will close this first part of my
response to the physiological objections still afloat on
this subject, and turn to the consideration of the
strongly-based conclusions of a number of able men
and women engaged at this moment in the work of
that higher education, the benefits of which have been
called in question.

PART V.

WHEREIN ARE GIVEN THE OPINIONS OF LEADING EDUCATIONISTS AS TO THE EFFECT OF THE MOVEMENT, WITH FURTHER STATISTICS.

V.

I CANNOT but think that the body of facts and responsible opinion I have been able to bring together, in dealing with this inquiry from the medical point of view, has done a good deal more than furnish even weight against the opinions which have been stated in an earlier section as held on the opposing side. But even so, I believe that, with the exception of the actual figures, this evidence will be seen to be of secondary importance to the combined experience of the large number of workers in the field of the higher education of women, whose interest in the cause has led them to furnish to this imperfect study, those observed results which I am now permitted to place before the reader.

In the persuasion that views formed on the basis of actual experience, of acquaintance with the student in her condition, not chiefly of disease, but of normal health, must be of higher value than any otherwise attainable in a calculation seeking to forestall the verdict of time, I endeavoured at the outset of this inquiry to obtain the witness at first hand of the most eminent and responsibly placed of those educationists who,

for the most part, are too busy in conducting the
actual work on the new lines to spare the time to lift
up their voices in its defence, or, perhaps, even to pay
much heed to its impugners.

To Miss Welsh, the Principal of Girton College, I
am indebted for the following :—

" The history of our students during the period
of their residence here and afterwards differs very
little, I think, as regards the physical side of their
lives, from that of other women of the same class.
In any respect in which it does differ, a distinct
improvement can, as a rule, be traced to the more
simple and regular habits acquired at college, and
to the widened mental and social interests which
have made life more full, and therefore more healthy
and happy.

" In the case of those who marry and have children, I have never heard of the slightest ill effect
traceable to the exceptional circumstances of their
education.

" The few instances of temporary overwork that
have come under my observation have in all cases
occurred in spite of, and not in consequence of, the
general tendency of the college life, and have been
caused more often by anxiety unconnected with work
than by the work itself."

Miss Clough, of Newnham College, sounds a less
confident note, but one full of instruction.   After
giving in her adhesion wholly to the speech of Sir

Spencer Wells at the opening of the Sanitary Association, she goes on to remark :—

" Young people must have some healthy interests, and they ought to be followed in moderation. If amusements are overdone, they do harm ; if too many hours are devoted to study, the students will suffer. I believe that periods of rest from severe intellectual pursuits—I may say, complete rest—are most valuable, and that rest between school and entering college is very desirable ; as also, that examinations should not be multiplied, especially when the students are under twenty. The Tripos examinations do fatigue women, but they also fatigue men. They have, however, their advantages : they rouse the intellect and cultivate energy and power of concentration ; they teach the students to express their knowledge in a short statement ; rapid thought is cultivated, and the power of making decisions quickly and seizing the golden opportunity. Some gentler qualities may, perhaps, be lost by the awakening of so much energy, but there are compensating advantages."

The next communication is that of Miss Wordsworth, of Lady Margaret Hall, Oxford :—

" In reply to your inquiry as to the effect of collegiate studies on the health of young women, I think I may say that everything depends—

" 1st, On their natural capabilities ; and,

" 2dly, On the moderation and good sense shown by themselves and their friends.

" It is worse than useless to send a girl of poor health, or neglected education, or mental sluggishness to an Oxford or Cambridge Hall, with the idea of making up for these deficiencies by her grinding at the subjects prescribed. The only effect is to make her physically ill and morally wretched, or else idle and indifferent; and experience has shown me that both these results are possible. Again, we have known instances of really clever girls, who, not being possessed of the moderation and good sense already spoken of, read an inordinate number of hours a day, sit up late, take little exercise, lose their appetites and nervous force, and fail where they might have succeeded, simply for want of self-control and resolute determination to observe the 'rule of not too much.'

" But when all these exceptions are made, I do not hesitate to say that, to sensible and clever girls, the life is a very beneficial one, as any life must be which enforces regular hours, simple meals, early rising, &c., and which affords cheerful companionship, games out of doors, and wholesome occupation for the mind. Much has been said about the victims of high pressure; something might be said, with at least equal truth, of the thousands of women who grow prematurely old in doing nothing; of the imaginary diseases of the unoccupied; of the idle, mischievous gossip, and irritability about trifles which characterise some rural and some suburban coteries; and still more might be urged in regard to the unwholesome excitements of fashionable life (which has slain its tens of thousands, where intellectual pursuits have slain, perhaps, their hundreds); and of the direct physical mischief caused by tight-lacing and other obvious absurdities. But I cannot close my letter without expressing my very sincere wish that study could be more for its own sake, and less with a view to examinations. I do not say that there should be *no* examinations, but that they should be fewer and easier. As they are now, they are the ruin of all true culture, mischievous in some cases to health, and do not show real ability or knowledge of a subject better than far simpler ones would do. Women, even more than men, in order to succeed in any pursuit, must love it. But how can any one love a thing that has to be 'crammed up' in a given number of weeks?

"You ask about the effect of intellectual training on the students' future as wives and mothers. So far as I know, there has been no material difference between the domestic history of collegiate students and that of their contemporaries in other spheres of life. There is no doubt that the craving for excitement in young girls often lasts on into the first decade of married life, and that the children of such parents are apt to be delicate. But my contention is that this craving for excitement is exactly what the *real* student, the lover of a subject for its own sake, is most likely to be free from. The rush into society, the restlessness of the empty-headed, is far more per-

H

nicious to home-life than the steady pursuits of one whose mind to him' (or her) 'a kingdom is.'"

I have not in all cases permission to give the names of those whose interest in the cause of education has inclined them thus generously to respond to my request for information. In adding their contributions, I will only premise that my correspondents, without exception, occupy responsible positions in the van of the higher education. One of these ladies writes :—

"As regards the health of students while at ——, I should say that those who *come* strong and well remain so. Some have come to us who have been delicate, and who we have considered should not have attempted the work; even these have, with care, been none the worse for it, and in several instances have even gained in strength. I could point to seven or eight who have thus decidedly improved in health."

From the letter of another I extract the following :—

"My own experience is that, so far from being injurious to girls, the present mode of education is distinctly beneficial to them, both morally and physically. Girls who have come to me so delicate that their friends have lived in constant anxiety about them, have in the majority of cases improved so much in health that the parents have lamented their not having been sent to a high school long before. The reasons are obvious : The life and the work are pleasant and bright; there is companionship, intellectual life, an atmosphere of genial sympathy, and a

certain amount of regular exercise necessitated by
these schools being day-schools. Above all, there is
definite interest and occupation, and hence the absence
of *dulness*, the scourge and bane (hitherto) of girls'
lives and the doctor's best ally; for girls of the upper
classes become ill from the utter stagnation of their
lives. . . . The published lists of University examinations show that women can do exactly the same
work as men, and compete successfully with them in
all branches of learning. At the Cambridge Senior
Local examination of 1885 one of our girls was the
best of all the candidates of either sex throughout the
Empire : she got distinction in Latin, Greek, German,
French, English, and Scripture.

" Some of my best and most hard-working girls
and teachers have been and are the daughters of
medical men, and no word of over-pressure have I
heard in their cases from their fathers, but, on the
contrary, a great deal of wholesome contempt for the
nonsense talked on the subject. . . . Dr. George
Buchanan's daughter is an M.A. of the University of
London ; the name of Dr. Chapnell's daughter appears
in the list of those who have successfully passed the
Cambridge examination."

To Miss Bulley I owe the ensuing :—

" I have known intimately Girton and Newnham
Colleges, and what is now the women's department of
Owen's College, Manchester. I have also had ten
years' experience at a high school for girls. I know

several families of children whose mothers were among
the *pioneers* of the movement now so savagely attacked.
In several directions, therefore, the effects of the
education of girls and women have been before me
from the very beginning of the movement. I hesitate
not in saying that, were an impression to get abroad
that a thorough school and college education is injurious to tolerably healthy girls and women, it would
be as mistaken as it would be unfortunate. I have
seen break-downs, but traced them in every case
either to disregard of reasonable moderation in study
or to original weakness of constitution, with which
prolonged study was incompatible without special care.
I have always found delicate girls more reckless than
strong and healthy ones. A college degree, like any
other course of training, needs a moderate basis of
strength, and any candidate with less must limit her
daily work rigorously. Satisfactory assurances of
health are now a necessary condition of holding
scholarships at several women's colleges. As to the
puny children that are said to owe their weakness to
over-educated mothers, I should like to know the
family constitution on both sides before deciding on
that point. I know, among my friends, not a few
sturdy, handsome children, whose mothers underwent
severe study in their earlier days. One of these was
a lady who, with one other, was the first woman to
take the Classical Tripos, and whose degree (second
class) was not beaten, I think, for ten years. In the

cases held up to us as 'awful warnings,' there was probably either constitutional weakness, or an insufficient time before marriage to recover from the temporary fatigue of college work and examinations.

"The strain on a teacher in a large school is very heavy, yet the regular hours, the steady occupation, and perhaps also the self-control which forms a necessary element in this life, exercise a stimulating effect upon the health. *If a better rate of payment removed money anxieties from the minds of teachers, we should probably have still better results.*

"There is a great temptation to the more eager spirits to overwork, and what is still worse, girls do not, as a rule, learn in what profitable study consists. They are occupied with books morning, noon, and night, and they think that if they pursue the same kind of life at college, they are doing the best that is possible. Their leisure should be carefully secured; let them not think that the addition of working hours necessarily means additional culture or even additional learning. For this purpose the *home*-work system needs reforming. We rely too much on this clumsy and antiquated weapon."

Miss Mackillip, of the Ladies' Collegiate School, Londonderry, has kindly supplied me, in addition to the statistics of the health of her pupils, which will be found in the Appendix, with the following result of her experience:—

"My unqualified testimony is, that if there is

reasonable care of the health of girls, the intellectual
quickening resulting from advanced education is of
great benefit to their physical condition.   I make the
health of the students the first consideration; ample
and good food, tennis, dancing, well-arranged hours
for study and exercise, and of all things, other interests besides learning, have done much to prevent
any ill effects from application to the latter.   One
test I constantly keep in view: if the girls are cheery,
as young girls should be, if joyousness is the prevailing tone, I have little fear that any bad result of
earnest and steady work will follow.   If, on the other
hand, I see a girl fretful, peevish, or over-anxious
about work, I feel it an imperative duty to stop the
study, or lessen it till the girl is in better tone.

"Perhaps it may be said that unusually robust girls
have fallen to my lot.   In any case, my experience is
exactly what I have stated; and as those I have noted
have nearly all been resident pupils, I speak with accurate
knowledge of their health.   I have taken for statistical
purposes only our most distinguished students.

"You will see by the results that the girls of the
school have done excellent work; and I have, as yet,
had no complaints of ill-health, weariness, or want of
vigour."

I now select the following from the testimony
rendered to the Schools Inquiry Commission by Miss
Buss, at present, and for many past years, the Principal of the North London Collegiate School.   It is the

only evidence I have cited which does not come to
me direct; but I have taken it since Miss Buss's
experience in the first clause strikes me as important
in showing how, in defiance of all truth, it is possible
to raise a scare.   Miss Buss says :—

"I think the difficulties on the ground of health of
the local examinations have been very much exag-
gerated.   The girls worked through the examination
in Manchester without any apparent fatigue or ill
effects.   I have since heard that some were carried
out fainting, and others in hysterics; but as I was
present, with the exception of five hours, during the
whole of the examination week, I can say from my
own personal knowledge that nothing of the kind
took place. . . . It seems to me that examinations
and endowments afford at the present moment the
best practical methods of improving female education.
We can only raise the education of the classes below
by beginning on the top."

I reserve to the last that which is the most detailed,
exact, and conclusive of the evidence which has been
placed at my disposal by the lady-educators, that, viz.,
of Miss Beale, the head of Cheltenham College.   Every
word of this veteran educationist is weighty, and my
only regret is that I am unable in this place to avail
myself of it more largely.   Miss Beale writes :—

"I have been head of this college for more than
twenty-eight years, during which time a complete
revolution has taken place in people's ideas about girls'

education.   Solid studies were then tabooed, so that,
though I had been at Queen's College the first lady-
mathematical tutor, I dared not at once introduce
mathematics here.   Even school examinations were
considered dangerous for girls ;   university examinations
were unheard of, and when these were proposed some
years later, the outcry was great.

" That the health of girls, moral, intellectual, and
physical, is immensely improved by the discipline and
intellectual training of a good education, is patent to
all who have to do with girls ; hysteria has almost
vanished.   Still from time to time cries are raised.

" In the general interests of education we have kept
the minutest possible statistics of our ten boarding-
houses, which have generally contained about 250
pupils.

" These show that girls, working under proper conditions, are *exceptionally* healthy.   I admit that some
evils are inseparable from examinations ; but the evils
of not examining work done are greater, and I think
that much of that incident to examination, is accidental
only.   The competition for scholarships and prizes,
the excitement of public speech-days, the working
whilst home anxieties press, trying to teach and learn
at once and to get the work of two years into one in
order to gain certificates, beginning to work late when
no foundation has been laid by early training, likewise
improper food and clothing, unsystematic arrangement
of time—these are the things that injure health and

bring discredit on education, for which it is in no way responsible.

"On hearing that an article was being written for a leading review, I thought I might help the cause by showing statistically how very large a proportion of those who had passed senior and higher university examinations had been in excellent health both before and after. If these had not suffered, *à fortiori* others would not.

"Our experience extends over more years than any large school except Miss Buss's. For some years, about half the women who passed the London University examination were prepared here. In all, during the last seventeen years, 627 pupils have passed senior and higher university examinations; in the early years very few cared to enter, and the large majority of those who have passed have done so in the last ten years.

"I sent out the following paper of questions, namely: 'Age at present; Dates of coming to and leaving college, and respective ages; Occupation since; If married, when? Number of children; Have any died? Is their health good? How long were you ill at college? From what cause? What illness since? Do you think your health suffered in any way from the examination?' I have had only a few weeks to gather these statistics, and have not asked those (about sixty) who are still pupils, to fill up the paper; they are all well. We have sent to every old pupil who was get-at-able and within reach. Great numbers are away, however, in

India and other distant lands ; and the missing
papers are chiefly those of married pupils.   We have
at present received about 380 papers; these I have
divided into six classes, say No. 1 to 6 :—

1. Consists of 96 pupils who have *never* been ill at college or
   since they left, and who affirm that they felt no ill effects
   from the examination work.
2. Of 103 pupils who had some form of children's disease,
   mumps, measles, &c., at college, but nothing attributable
   to work, and *they have had no illness since.*
3. Of 16 pupils who had never been ill at college, but have
   had some unimportant illness since ; they also affirm to
   no ill effects from work.
4. Of 14 pupils who went out of their way, *though unasked,* to
   say study had benefited their health.   This class would
   have been much larger had it occurred to me to ask the
   question.
5. Of 100 pupils who had had some illness in college and
   some since, but had in no way suffered from the work.
6. Among 54 pupils who gave a more or less unfavourable
   answer, I have placed all who gave the slightest hint
   that they might have suffered.   The greater number
   of these, say 35, answered in such terms as 'Slightly,'
   'Friends think not quite so well,' 'No permanent ill
   effects,' 'Perhaps a little,' &c., &c.   Of the remaining
   29, some could not have suffered seriously, as they were
   never ill since ; some studied for examination whilst
   teaching ; some suffered from the combination of study
   and *home anxieties;* some were very delicate when they
   came, and of a delicate family ; and some suffered from
   causes the details of which I cannot publish, as the particular case might be recognised.

" Speaking of the list generally, I may say that in some
few cases at least, the difficulty of preparing to answer
examiners was complicated by that of deciding what

reply should be given to a question more important
than those asked by professors of classes and mathematics ; one which is not usually answered with perfect
calmness, whether it be yes or no.   Some who have
suffered, came late to us, and felt it of great importance to their future to pass an examination.   Some
were induced by their friends to risk it in a time
shorter than what was needed.

" Thus more than half of our examinees during
seventeen years have had *no illness at all* since they left,
and one-fourth none either at college or since.   Of Class
I, the respective ages of the pupils are as follows :—

53	of	from	17	to	22
35	„	„	23	„	27
12	„	„	28	„	30
3	„	„	34	„	38

The stay at college of most of them has been from
about 2 to 3, of some from 4 to 5, and of several up to
9 and 10 years.

" In conclusion, I have done what I can with regard to
the married women, but, unfortunately for my statistics,
very many are in distant countries, so that I have only
papers from 40 pupils of the ages of from 22 to 29 and
some up to 34 years.   Of these, 8 have been married
one year or less and have no children ; of those married
one year or longer, only 3 are childless.   The rest give
an aggregate of 97 years, and have had 42 children,
of which 39 are living, and their health is reported as
follows :—' Excellent,' ' Remarkably good,' ' Very good '

for 11, 'Good' for 25, and 'Fairly good' for 3, but
who were born in India.

"The labour I have undertaken has brought me
many interesting letters from our pupils, and useful
suggestions.   The standard of health has certainly
risen with the introduction of improvements.   Proper
gymnasiums, superior boarding-houses, large gardens
and tennis-courts, the avoidance of extraneous excitement, of the giving of prizes by *competition*, and of
having speech-days, and of publishing class-lists.   We
cannot altogether prevent overwork amongst day-girls,
if parents will not let us know, but we send home an
evening time-table, and request to be informed if the
time is exceeded.   Often we refuse to let girls learn
as many things as their parents wish."

With these excerpts from the evidence of the
principals of those colleges or high schools which I
have taken as typical, I will quote a passage from
a letter of Miss Gurney, whose large experience lies
upon a lower plane of educational requirement, which
has yet not escaped charges of over-pressure.   Miss
Gurney writes :—

"I have had very little to do with college-work.
As far as school-work is concerned, my belief is that
the dangers to the health of girls from regular study
are far less than the dangers from listlessness and
want of training of the mental powers.   Study is
very easy to girls of average ability, when it is begun
early and on good methods, and especially when it is

combined with exercise and careful physical training, so that the body is trained with the mind. I think we must consider that intellectual advantages are definitely opened to women now. They have been put within the reach of girls, who have seized upon them so eagerly that there can be no backward step. The great point for people like ourselves, who have to do with the management of schools, is to keep a careful watch that the best methods are used (for example, to keep down the time spent on writing and preparation), and also to put forward physical training. On the question of overwork, we want the co-operation of parents. With this view we have printed forms in our high schools limiting hours of preparation, which parents are required to sign."

I have given precedence to the testimony of women in this portion of the examination of that which, while it concerns the whole human race, is primarily a woman's question—one vitally affecting the whole future of woman, social, domestic, and economic ; and thus I have reserved to the last the evidence of so great an authority on education as Mr. Fitch, one of Her Majesty's Inspectors of Training Schools throughout the kingdom. It is in the nature of things that his experience, though not deeper, takes a wider sweep than that of the principals and mistresses of colleges and schools.

"There is, to my thinking," writes Mr. Fitch, " no doubt that when people are in earnest about any pursuit, whether it be the pursuit of learning or of

pleasure, or any other object of human ambition, there
will be danger of occasional over-exertion.   It is part
of the price we pay for having any good work or noble
effort in the world at all.   But the real question at
issue is: have the new facilities which of late have
been afforded to women for the attainment of sounder
knowledge and more serious and varied intellectual
employment, tended to increase disease and weakness,
and to diminish in any way the happiness of women's
lives?   And to this question I am sure the right
answer is an emphatic negative.   Evidence in favour
of a negative conclusion is, however, always hard to
give; but I know of no evidence on the other side,
although, if such evidence existed, it would be easy of
proof.   There is much vague and conjectural statement
in the writings of opponents, but, so far as I have been
able to judge, no facts to justify their apprehensions.
The wisest physicians and teachers I have known are
agreed in believing that mental discipline and exertion
are great helps to healthy physical development; that
the greatest curses of young-ladyhood are listlessness,
vacuity of mind, and the lack of serious purpose, and
of interesting and useful occupation.   For one person
whose health has been injured by intellectual ambition
and effort, I believe there are fifty who have been far
more seriously injured by frivolity, by mental idleness,
and by indifference to the cultivation of their higher
faculties.   So I have no doubt whatever that every
encouragement lately given to the pursuit of learning

by the universities, every new high school for girls
which has been started, and every new opening that
has been made for women to professional employment
and to honourable public work, has been a distinct
gain to the community, and has added as much to
the health of women, as a class, as it has undoubtedly
added to the number of their intellectual interests, and
the enjoyment and usefulness of their lives. But this,
of course, is a mere general statement of opinion, and
needs, as you will say, to be verified." Mr. Fitch then
suggests that application should be made for the direct
experience of the ladies, mistresses of colleges and high
schools, the fruitful results of which I have, at the risk
of iteration, laid before the reader. After expressing
his belief that the women-students who have married,
will have carried into domestic life more power of exercising a right and beneficent influence over their families
and friends than they would have possessed had they
enjoyed a less generous education, he proceeds :—

  " I may add, that my own duties give me special
opportunities of looking at the problem from another
point of view. There are in England twenty-six training colleges for schoolmistresses, containing in all 1800
resident students. It is my duty, on behalf of the
Government, to make an annual visit to these institutions, and I have seen every one of them during the
last twelve months. Among other things, it is needful
that I inquire carefully of the medical officer of each
college respecting the health of the students. I may

say that all of these students are between the ages of
eighteen and twenty-one, that they are being trained
for a laborious profession, and that their time in college
is passed in systematic study, and in practice in the
art of teaching.   At the end of each year they are
examined under the regulations of the Education Department, in order that they may receive certificates
qualifying them to become teachers in elementary
schools.   Now here, if there were any danger to
young women in a life of regular mental application,
the evil would show itself.   But the testimony of the
medical officers is remarkably favourable.   Cases of
failure in health are exceedingly rare, and many of the
largest colleges have, during five or six successive years,
escaped the necessity of parting with a single pupil
from this cause.   Moreover, it is the uniform opinion
of the medical officers that the students improve in
health and vigour during their two years of residence ;
and this opinion is strongly confirmed by my own observations of the demeanour and appearance of the
young people, and of the interest they show in their
work.   So while it may be admitted that great watch-
fulness is needed as to the working of modern experi-
ments in improving the education of women, I believe
you will find that the balance of experience and trustworthy testimony is enormously in favour of such
movements. . . . I should regard any discouragement
to the cause of the higher education of women in England as a serious public misfortune."

It was my purpose, in dealing with the authorities friendly to the higher culture of women, to have subjected their statements to the same examination as I had used in regard to those of its opponents ; but in surveying them with this view, I find so studious a measure observed in them, with such a determination to yield all that is clearly indefensible in the position taken up, that little or no advantage seems allowed to attack. No one will deny to educationists filling such prominent and distinguished positions, the opportunity of becoming practically acquainted with the facts to which they testify ; and it will be seen also that their observations, drawn from facts with which they have daily to deal, are conducted neither on foreign soil exposed to confusing extraneous conditions, nor have reference to a state of things which the rapid pace of modern progress has rendered obsolete ; but have been drawn from and apply to contemporary England, and are records of the best opinion of the day, almost, it may be said, of the hour. That the opinions of the educationists here cited should be mainly those of women, can hardly be held to take from their weight, since in the education of women, women are naturally the experts ; but some deduction may possibly be justly claimed from any, the most impartial testimony delivered from the point of view of those who have embarked their energies in a given work. One point must be clear to all who have read the words of these practical educationists with any attention : they are as fully alive as the most solicitous of the outside world

I

can be to the danger to be feared from over-pressure, and are generally opposed, as well in the interests of culture *per se* as in those of health, to the magnified proportions which the system of competitive examination has taken in modern education.

It does not come within the scope of my design, in this slight review of a wide subject, to advance any personal opinion in regard to the particular lines on which the higher education of women is now conducted.

Much that relates to method is, in the present stage of the movement, only tentative, and its effects are, without doubt, being studiously watched by the earnest and able women who are engaged in the conduct of this new intellectual departure.

That the generally acknowledged inferiority of the sex in those qualities of reason, judgment, and (to some limited extent of) self-control, which the more solid education of men has been supposed to favour, should have led in the first instance to a trial of similar educational means in the case of girls, is only natural as an initial step. If experience shall hereafter show that some divergence in method or in choice of subjects of study, is better calculated to elicit the hidden treasure of feminine capacity, and to fit the more heavily tried half of human kind for that battle of life from which, in large numbers, they are not exempted, there need be no fear that the change of plan will fail to be carried into effect in due time.

I have now stated the case for either side of this contention with as much completeness as my limited

plan will permit, and thus presented, it appears
sufficiently clear to dispense with any elaborate sum-
ming up on my part. It is, in the first place, apparent
that the increased facilities for the advanced education
of girls is a wide-spread fact, and it is equally indis-
putable that the alarm raised from time to time by
remonstrants from without, finds no echo in the minds
of those who are the responsible conductors of the
movement.   That the competitive system, impugned
by many of the best authorities on education, male and
female, presses harder on women than on men, may be
likewise gathered. If the female organism bears the
wear and tear of life on the whole as well or better
than that of the male, there is little doubt that the
latter is possessed of more force available at a given
time for a given effort. This is a disadvantage with
which female educationists have to reckon, and one
to which, as it will be seen, they appear fully alive.
The sounder methods upon which girls are now being
taught, the freer ventilation of class-rooms, the more systematic balancing up of the body against the mind, have
solved many difficulties, and increased experience of the
special requirements of girls in matters wherein they
may be found to differ from boys, may be expected to
solve many more.   Any attempt in this place to prove
that the aptitudes of the female mind are almost im-
measurably greater than they were believed to be by
our forefathers, would be mere waste of words ; the
record of average achievement in the years during
which they have competed at examinations furnishing

substantial proof of their equality with men in matters
of mere acquirement.

Thus, then, this necessarily slight review of the
case as it stands, is offered to the candid consideration
of the reader. The final verdict as to how far the
movement, in its inevitable march, will conduce to
the well-being of the race, must be left to the fulness of time; but such words of this sentence as have
already dropped from the oracle, may be taken as
affording bright promise to the harvest of the future.
In view of my circumscribed object, I have regarded what is known as overstrain in education, solely
in relation to the advanced culture of pupils of the
weaker or gentler sex. That the public mind has also
been occupied with the too-frequent evil effects of
even primary education upon the impoverished physical
constitutions of children, boys no less than girls, taken
from the lowest stratum of society, I am of course
aware; but as such education is only felt to be hard
work by reason of conditions which all may hope are
in part remediable, which no one would claim as
inhering in the nature of things, and as, moreover, it
bears equally on both sexes, it has not seemed to me
to come within the scope of this examination.

I must now take leave to carry the question of the
fitness of women for a higher kind of work than has
yet been allotted to them (still seen from the physiological side) from that limited ground of preparation
for life from which we have thus far regarded it, into
the wider sphere of life itself.

PART VI.

*IN WHICH THE CASE OF WOMEN IN THEIR
NEW RELATION TO WORK IS FINALLY
RESUMED.*

VI.

"What shall arrive with the cycle's change ?
A novel grace and a beauty strange."—BROWNING.

WHEN from the point of preparation for life and its
allotted work we extend our glance into the limitless
field of life itself, we find that whatever may be urged
of the necessity of guarding from undue pressure the
nascent powers of the young, the lot of the toiling
millions all over the earth, is to be overworked. It is
thus in the mines and the mills ; it is thus in garrets
and cellars ; thus scarcely less with the over-driven
mothers of numerous poverty-stricken families than
with the lonely semptresses, shirtmakers, tailoresses,
and others, at work for twelve and fourteen hours of a
day which scarcely suffices to supply them with the
food needful to keep them in life. The bent backs
and splay feet of our farm-labourers attest the fact as
well as the varicose veins and mesenteric disorders of
the women who serve in shops, and the wizened coun-
tenances observable in every crowd which brings us
face to face with the labouring poor. This stringency
of effort is by no means confined to one sex or to any
class. All high ambitions, impersonal or other, are

apt to demand it ; all passionate dedication to learning or art, or the service of man. And the lot of those men or women who win their bread by the toil of the brain can be expected to offer no immunity from this sweat of the brow, this overtasking of the powers, in which labour bears the aspect of a primal curse to millions of our fellow-creatures, the victims of circumstances which allow them no more choice of its kind than of its degree.

What I wish to establish by the foregoing reflections is, that it would be impossible of proof, and in the highest degree improbable *per se*, that severe bodily exertion, longer endured for worse pay, offers less danger to health than a correspondent mental expenditure made under happier conditions and for more adequate reward. Also, that the brain labour for which the subject yielding it has been duly trained, is likely to be less exhausting than that with which the poor candidates for the Governess' Benevolent Annuity have had to struggle, commonly without any preparation at all. For it must be borne in mind, when considering the aptness of women for severe intellectual exercise, that the choice of the working woman of the better classes, is not between brain labour and the comparative ease of what has been conventionally known as " woman's sphere," but between brain labour methodised and lightened by suitable education, and brain labour on which they are thrust in the helplessness and confusion of ignorance ; or, when not that, of manual labour, which implies a loss of social status, and for which very often they are physically unfit. For, as has been pointed out, not the most piteous of the pleas for the protection of the female mind from overstrain, can ever be backed by a promise or prospect of getting the work of these compassionated ones done for them by champions of the sex which is supposed alone capable of performing it victoriously, even if there were not presumably a growing difficulty to be contended with on the head of marriage, in that more individualised requirement of the cultivated woman which makes it the less easy for her to fit herself with a mate.

In the meanwhile, the subjects of this over-tender interest must live, and there is a feeling among them, also growing and gathering force, that they have a right to live by such means, and to live as well as the best use of their faculties, small or great, will allow them.

By what right, it may reasonably be asked, should thousands of responsible beings be forced to put up with the lower rewards of manual labour or intellectual incompetence, when consciously possessed of powers in whose exercise they might find pleasure as well as profit ? If women are in ever-increasing numbers driven to their own resources for a living, and if the few traditional callings open to them in the past have become blocked by competition to the point that entrance on any terms is to the bulk of applicants

denied, it follows that new openings for their energies,
mental or bodily, must be sought for. The practice
which once obtained in China of condemning female
infants to death at the hour of birth, if apparently
more brutal, would in effect be less cruel than any
arbitrary interference with the economic conditions on
which lonely and struggling women are seeking to
earn their bread. If already an army of women of
the humbler class has forced its way by gradual pressure into manual employments from which they were
formerly excluded, there is a large contingent of the
better born and more delicately nurtured, thrown
upon its own efforts for existence—women whose
status, abilities, and reasonable claims make the lower
forms of labour repugnant. For it is coming at
length to be frankly confessed by women and better
understood by men, that even the most ideal creature
of the gentler sex, if having to battle for herself, is
not so necessarily devoid of all personal ambition as it
has been the delight of male romancists to represent
her, but is, on the contrary, reasonably sensible of a
desire to use, of her faculties, just those which are
likely to bring her the best return not only in money
but in social consideration. The flattery which has
assumed such selflessness, such readiness of sacrifice
to no adequate end, on the part of women, though a
delicate tribute, has cost them dear. These women-
workers, then, of the higher social class, have pressed,
and must continue to press, even as their humbler

sisters, against barriers which must crush them if they do not to some extent yield. To them a variety of callings, demanding more or less of culture and intelligence, are gradually being opened; and to the necessity which is driving girls to fit themselves for such, much, most of the new impulse to female education is attributable. Something has to be risked on the part of parents whose children are so placed as to be compelled to earn their bread. The preparation for the work of life must be begun early if the fight is not to prove harder than need be to the end.

Patent, however, as is the fact that the sphere in which the cultivated woman of to-day may hope to exercise her faculties is steadily enlarging, the reports of the colleges and high schools show that the profession of teaching, lifted to a higher plane, and in answer to increasing demands, is that which still attracts the vast majority of qualified women. Few callings, there is reason to believe, make greater demands upon the nervous energies; few callings could probably show more cases of break-down among men. But the modern woman-teacher, better prepared for her better systematised work, shows well as compared with her male competitor, triumphantly as compared with the governess of olden days.

The little book issued yearly containing the list of the candidates for the Governesses' Benevolent Annuity, and setting forth their claims, is the saddest reading conceivable. Of the hundreds of poor ladies sufficiently befriended to institute a canvass for this charity, most have entered upon their career early and probably ill-equipped, and have supported others than themselves on the miserable pittance it has brought them. All have broken down in health and been rendered incapable by the age of fifty or sixty, and at the time of appeal are in bitterest need. Paralysis, trouble of the vocal organs, and blindness—diseases of the over-taxed and lonely—are the forms in which infirmity has chiefly overtaken them. Such a record of wasted life and energy is enough to strike sadness to the hardest heart. And yet this annual record has been in the hands of a large number of persons for over fifty years, and it has seemed not to have occurred to a benevolent public, lay or professional, to disturb itself with the reflection that, under that old system of female education and employment which still finds advocates, such was the only future prepared for the daughters of needy gentry. All else was matter of chance, dependent upon welcome opportunities of marriage.

I may be permitted in this place to draw upon the small sum of my own personal experience in further illustration. Dining, or rather supping, lately at one of the halls of residence for female students of the London University, I could not fail to remark the happiness and health of the faces crowding the several tables, or, while admiring the ample justice done to the excellent fare provided, to feel my own spirits lifted by the moral atmosphere which prevailed, impregnated as it seemed by the buoyancy and elasticity of youthful hope.

When, later in the evening, we retired to the drawing-room, it so happened that of the dozen or fourteen young ladies present, two were doctors in practice, and the rest were for the most part medical students. I must allow that I felt a difference in the manners of these young women from those at present prevailing in what is called society, but it was not in the direction that many would seem to expect. They were less restless, more gentle and womanly, with not a trace in their language or in their, in some cases, carefully considered dress, of the fastness and loudness with which conscious inferiority is wont to proclaim itself. I was able to pursue my observations more critically and in detail than in the refectory, and looked at the young ladies severally with a view to finding out indications of over-tasked strength, well knowing that such were to be sought for, if anywhere, in the students of a profession for which the preliminary examinations are above all severe. My eyes passed over face after face without discovering traces of fatigue, although one young Mistress of Arts had had to support herself by teaching while reading for her degree. By the time, however, that I had finished my survey, two had separated themselves from the rest, and dwelt in my mind as offering something more than doubtful cases of over-taxed power. I could not help remarking to my neighbour that clearly the constitutions of those two young ladies had not been equal to the demand made upon them. When I was told in reply that the two I had picked out as victims of over-strain were *nurses* who were suffering from the wear and tear of that universally admitted womanly calling, and were in consequence about to fit themselves for general practice as *doctors*, I own I experienced a considerable reinforcement of the opinions I had already seen occasion to form upon the subject.

There is no doubt that the odds and ends of necessary work, the " leavings," with which women have heretofore been content, have not been allotted to them as the lightest, any more than as the most profitable, of the labour of the world. But I will leave the foregoing illustrations to point their own moral.

Granting, as we must if we fairly face the facts, that the new forms in which the burthen of life are being accepted by the weaker sex are rather laid upon its needier members than chosen by them, of what avail are such questions as that of Dr. Withers Moore as to " whether it be well that our women should be equipped and encouraged to enter the battle of life shoulder to shoulder and on equal terms with men " ? We know too well that in ever-increasing numbers they have to enter into the battle, whether they like it or not. The question, thus so far settled for us, resolves itself into the simpler one of *terms*. Shall women be driven to the fight, in which no allowance will be made for their heavier burthens, *un*equipped and *dis*couraged—the disadvantages inherent in sex being set up as the starting-point for increased and arbitrary disabilities ? or shall the terms of contract be made as equal as the peculiarities of the case permits ?

I think there is so much, if not of justice, then of gentleness and mercy, (much commoner qualities) in the world, that the question will not long remain in doubt.

As we have seen, the ground on which a right has been assumed to interfere with the economic employment of women's time and powers is that of the health and progressive development of the race. Without ignoring the gravity of this aspect of the contention, it is sufficiently clear that the defences with which, in this regard, it has been sought to surround the sex, are not so much inadequate to the end as positively subversive of it. The gentlemen who from time to time have pronounced so glibly on the tendency of the intellectual culture of women to deteriorate the race, have surely not duly considered the weight of the embargo they would lay upon women's lives; to what poverty, poor feeding, mean employment unmercifully prolonged, and, worse than all, to what temptation they would consign them in hopeless thousands. It may be said that those upon whom such a doom would fall, would not be the women chosen to become the mothers of future generations; but the heart revolts against such callous comfort, and the faith in the Unseen Power that works for righteousness, assures us that heavy reprisals would be exacted for cruelty and waste so reckless. Not to go farther, we may see how, in such a state of things, the weak, the venal, and consciously incompetent, would crowd the marriage market, and possess themselves of the limited supplies to be found in it, while the braver, truer, and more progressive spirits went empty upon their way. The survival of the fittest does not always imply the survival of the best : in this case it would be the survival of the basest.

It may be hoped, however, that the evidence produced in the foregoing pages, to the effect that intellectual work, with its preliminary training, if conducted on reasonable lines, is not injurious to the health of averagely healthy women, will have had some influence in shaping hitherto unformed convictions ; and the position contended for being admitted, it may fairly be inferred that such work is not necessarily prejudicial to the health of offspring. In the absence of fuller statistic on this latter point (that which exists being wholly confirmatory), the inference deduced from such a postulate may be allowed to hold its own against the loose affirmations of the accusing side.

The path of independence in which women are now seeking their way, has become for them the path of duty. If the strictest obligation of the individual, from whom the first natural supports have fallen away and are not replaced by others, is to provide for its own existence, it may possibly come to pass that, by the free use of the highest means available to this end, the larger, more recondite result of advantage to the race, will follow.

I will not dwell at any length upon the unfairness, where the difficulties of the individual are so great, of laying the whole strain of duty to the race upon that half of it which has the least choice in bringing its members into existence. Yet it must be acknowledged that it is pressing somewhat too hardly upon women, whose personal volition has relatively so little influence on their election as wives, to be required at great sacrifice to maintain themselves at the level supposed to be best suited to the performance of that maternal function which for many will for ever remain inactive. Granting what has been shown in an earlier section to be clearly possible, that a high expenditure of brain-power may detract from fertility in the sense here spoken of (and that with either sex, the male no less than the female), it would be impossible to maintain, on anything less than the assumption that women were the born slaves of men, that the right of the one sex to develop itself in accordance with its highest capacity, was less than that of the other. When it comes to settling in what that highest capacity consists, the experience of the subject who feels the pressure of the impulse guiding and shaping all life, from the seaweed upwards, can alone be taken as decisive. We are often crudely told that the noblest office of woman is to swell the census returns; but the command to increase and multiply falls with continually

K

less force upon our older civilisations, and the spiritual quickening which is felt as the throb of a new life, and a higher, more impersonal hope, by the more progressive minds throughout the world, is, as has elsewhere been said, a new departure in the history of human progress—one of those upheavals against which, when occurring in their appointed time, all puny, merely mortal effort is unavailing.

Moreover, should we still insist on regarding the woman solely from the point of view of the mother of men, it cannot be satisfactorily maintained, that the part of the female progenitor is so paramount in importance as to make it advisable that the whole weight of supposed duty to the race shall be saddled upon her. What, apart from the strain of legitimate effort, from which in our over-crowded arena men also must suffer, might not be urged of the cases in our teeming hospitals of rickety, scrofulous, and otherwise afflicted children, whose misery, impartial science informs us, is mainly due to the animal indulgence to which the stronger sex is admittedly the more prone? What, too, apart from vicious excess, of the prevalence among youths at the most critical stage of development, of the inordinate use of tobacco? It would need to be shown very clearly that the condition of the mother was indeed so vastly more important than that of the father to the well-being of progeny, before society could be warranted in taxing the efforts of women for honourable independent existence, with restrictions which have never yet been proposed in regard to the worst vices of men.

It may here be pertinently asked, to what point in the imaginary interests of the race would the education of young women require to be degraded from that in practice during the first period of the movement for its advance, and affirmed then by alarmists to be dangerously in excess of female requirement ?

What if it should appear that the function performed with exemplary regularity by a cow, could be most efficiently exercised by a human mother whose brain as regards culture was a blank ; and most uninterruptedly by one whose emotional nature was also in a slumbrous condition ?   Such a position is certainly not wholly untenable ; but what then ?   Were it well in such case that the untransferable, not to be substituted ministrations of the human parent, should be sacrificed to a few months of more perfect accomplishment of an office with which the advance of science has shown it possible largely to dispense ?   This would be poor economy of means, seeing that the moral and spiritual influence of the mothers of mankind, is felt over the whole of life.

Looking beyond the moment and the individual to the cumulative masses of humanity in the future, if the cultured woman is indeed found to be unfertile as compared with her neglected sisters, the circumstance could hardly be regarded as a grave menace by those who are living in view of the dangers and difficulties of over-population in our great centres. Of far other significance would be any evidence that could be confirmed, of a deterioration in the quality, mental or physical, of the human stock produced by educated mothers; but although, as we have seen, the facts in possession may not as yet amount to irrefragable proof, there is ground for the strongest presumption that the direct reverse of this is the case. Over and above the few figures which have been collected to this end, will any one of average experience venture to affirm, that the children of the unlettered poor are more vigorous during their early years, and of larger stature, better developed, and more apt for learning as they advance, than those of the professional or aristocratic classes? This is so notoriously not the fact, that we are justified in inferring that if some modification in fecundity is a common result, not only of mental over-strain, but of a more equable distribution of energy throughout the system, deterioration in the quality of offspring is the distinctive mark of excessive bodily labour.

Thus we see that the counsellors who are so solicitous for the welfare of women as mothers of the race, have taken too narrow a view of the complicated situation, and would do well to reflect upon the straits to which arbitrary interference with economic conditions or liberty of development, would drive the subjects of their care. In denying the power of natural expansion to the sphere of the struggle in which so many must engage, they could not fail to surcharge it with

conditions more baleful alike to health of body and
mind than any from which they could aspire to free
it. It cannot be too often repeated, until it is fairly
laid to heart, that hard and continuous hand-labour,
poorly paid as such labour mostly is, and becoming
worse by hungry competition, may be reckoned on,
when coupled with the bad and insufficient food which
such toil is able to supply, to wear out the worker
more surely and miserably than the equally hard effort
of a better-fed brain. Not to bring so great a word
as "justice" into a connection from which it would
appear to have a natural estrangement, if women are
unable, in one shape or another, to hold themselves
aloof from the competition and the strain, common
humanity demands that liberty shall be allowed
them in determining the direction of their energies,
and that being often forced to spend themselves
unduly, they shall not also be driven to spend themselves for nought. In other words, that those who
may be called upon to give up something of health
and well-being in the struggle for life, shall be free to
take their commodity to the best market. We hear
nothing in this contention of the cases which abound
in the purlieus of our great cities, of women suffering,
dying, from serum of the brain consequent on continuous needlework; or of the insanity which the
tables of lunacy inform us is especially frequent among
maids-of-all-work. Very possibly such women may, in
large numbers, be competent at a certain period of

their career, to contribute their full quota to our overflowing census returns; but it would be hard to see how this probable enrichment of our hospitals, workhouses, or prisons, would in any way benefit the nation at large. The prizes of life in the sphere of work, manual or other, are the award of intelligence (when such can obtain fair-play); and if working women are to have their due share in them, it can only be through trained ability in the use of faculty.

As a side issue, the state of things known in America as the "man-famine," exists in far larger proportion among ourselves. Shall we dare to take upon us, if such a thing were possible, to annul or retard by artificial means, the reaction against some of its worst consequences which is being prepared by Nature?

If marriage is removed beyond the reach of thousands of women who would joyfully accept its conditions, should we not at least beware of increasing what to many must be the hardship of its denial, by the mockery of fitting women alone for its ends?

The increased stir of the intellectual faculties of the retarded sex, is a great fact of evolution which is being ushered in by means of customary severity. Any successful attempt to interrupt its progress, for however short a time, by the cultivation, through idleness and the sickness of hope deferred, of a class of feelings to which legitimate expansion is largely denied, could only tend to the degradation of the sex so tampered with from without.

The adjustments of Nature are delicate and subtle
beyond our utmost power of divination. It behoves
us to confine our endeavours to steadying its course of
progress, or at most, if venturing to suggest its direction, to do so with the reverence, not to say the
timidity, that beseems our ignorance.

On the whole, the freedom which every noble race
has worked out for its sons, must be counted on as
the best guarantee for the corresponding development
of its daughters.

Freedom! yes, freedom; the word must be spoken—
the word which is writ large upon every banner of
progress throughout the world. Moral and spiritual
forces are everywhere gaining ground; "*les races se
feminisent.*" The right of the strongest has no longer
the sacredness of natural law; is in less danger of
being taken for the right divine. The subjection of
women must have an end.

It is nothing less than a change of view which is
demanded of our generation. Woman, rehabilitated by
single-handed labour and the responsibility of her own
existence, is slowly emerging from her state of tutelage.
To the toiling and groaning, almost starving millions,
the women at work in garrets and cellars, we, the
children of ease, the shielded and cared for, owe a
debt we can never adequately repay. They it is who
form the mass which is urging forward our too often
heedless steps, goaded themselves by the demon of
famine and all the temptations of despair. Let us not

forget those seemingly God-forgotten ones who are working, if blindly, to ends which of ourselves we could never have reached. Many are doomed to perish, giving up the fight in utter weariness. We call them fallen. They are not fallen ; they are thrown down in the struggle, cast into the mire, and ruthlessly trampled upon ! The shame which in their debasement can scarcely reach them, is ours, not theirs. We owe them more than tears for the freedom they are helping us to work out; for opening our eyes to the criminal side of a system in which we have thoughtlessly acquiesced. To those who stand in a conflict so fierce, our strongest support is due ; to those who are down, our tenderest regard.

It is the emancipation of women, then, from the absolutism, the leading, and from what is too often the tyranny of man, which is the meaning of the new activity that is everywhere at work. The dual power which has always been felt throughout the whole of life, will attain to more perfect balance. The *Ewige Wiebliche*, though no new force in the world, will be lifted to its proper sphere. The woman, ceasing to be a mere queen-consort, as in the old ideal, will become a queen-regnant, bound to no taskwork, but acting in accordance with a rule from within—the true helper and complement of man, reigning no longer solely by his grace, but by the grace of God.

That there is need for this lifting up and *humanising* of the woman's position, must be clear to all who have ever thought of the ordinary life of an ordinary woman as a whole : the short day of youth, in which, if sufficiently attractive, she is courted, and the long years whereof each one takes something from her personal consideration and regard.

It is well that something of the individualism which is helping to work out the modern idea of progress, should have come to assert itself among women, and that they should at last feel it not impossible to crown their lives with honour not solely derived from men.

Hear for a moment the view taken of the status of women in the politest nation in Europe, at the close only of the last century. I quote the words of Diderot :—

"Time advances, beauty passes; then come the years of neglect, of spleen, of weariness. It is in pain that Nature disposes them for maternity ; in pain and illness, dangerous and prolonged, she brings maternity to its close. What is a woman after that ? Neglected by her husband, left by her children, a nullity in society, then piety becomes her one and last resource."

This, with some exception for superior character, ability, or good fortune, is the social order, well according with the condition of the law and of public opinion, from which the sex has been gradually emerging. That it was possible in the eighteenth century, in that France wherein female influence was most acknowledged, to propound a view of the status of women so fundamentally contemptuous, must surely point the moral that women are now doing well and wisely in enlarging for themselves a life based on other than material ends. Over and above the struggle for exist-ence and the desire for knowledge on its own account, it is the claim of a common humanity that women are now pressing. The best of them refuse to regard themselves as the ephemera of a day of beauty, to be swept to oblivion on the tide of man's scorn when their work of physical increase is accomplished. That Nature is cruel must be admitted; but every step in social progress is a step beyond Nature. The correction of its brutalities is the first truly human work of life.

It was remarked to me lately, that "the women who ruled India had been, not the beautiful sultanas, the first favourites, but plain, and very often old women —hags, as, under such circumstances, the deposed are sure to become. Not to go into the question of how far it is true that any women, beautiful or ugly, young or old, have "ruled India," we might all be quite pre-pared to learn that the Light of the Harem was not necessarily a potent influence. She is too much the creature of her lord for it to be worth his while to go far out of his way to humour her caprices. Is she not his at all hazards, living in his life, and dying, socially at least, at his death? The woman who wins the ear of the despot, is naturally one in whom love of power and joy in the exercise of cunning, have taken the place of the petty passions of her youth, and who feels an irresponsible pleasure in playing upon the lower chords

of the man's nature, and leading him by flattery and
cajolery, to advance or overthrow the puppets of the
political game in accordance with the motives which
rule in her narrow sphere. Far other is the influence,
nurtured by freedom, by knowledge, and community of
interest, that is now preparing ; far other is the status
which will be that of the true helpmate of man when
the world, which has still so much to accomplish in
the interests of the race, shall be no more one-handed.

It may appear to some persons that too much promi-
nence has been given in this study, to the agency of
the growing necessity of work as a means of existence
in developing the movement which has been under
discussion.

I believe myself that it is scarcely possible to exag-
gerate the force of this element of propulsion ; that
we have to acknowledge in it the whip and goad by
which all mortal inertia is overcome, and accepted
tyrannies rebuked and ultimately delivered from ;
that, in short, it is nothing less than the unseen
power—that " other " of the Gospel, which, the fulness of time being come, is " girding " the belated
pilgrim of life, and leading her " whither " of herself
she " would not."

But while acknowledging the driving force of circumstances in setting the movement afloat, we can never
afford to forget that the object of all education worthy of
the name, is twofold—an *enrichment* of the life of the
subject, and an *equipment* or qualifying for a success-

ful life-work.* Although more stress may be laid on one
or other of these terms, in accordance with individual
needs, the dual work should never be wholly separated.

When all is said on the side of the question which
deals with equipment for the struggle of life, it is
impossible too strongly to repudiate opinions, such as
are sometimes broached in the course of this discussion,
to the effect that the whole outlay of a woman's college
education, conducted at great expense, is of " no avail "
if its possibly primary purpose of bread-winning has
been missed through marriage. Again, the notion of
education must be rigidly contracted, and even warped,
when it is found possible to aver that it " comes under
the head of waste " unless a life is devoted to its practical use, and when it is spoken of as being " no gain "
to the mother of a family. Since one of the high, if
not the highest of educational aims, is " the cultivation
of the judgment, and the discouragement of the habit
of concluding hastily on insufficient premises," there is
no walk of life in which systematic training could be
" no gain," and few in which the gain would be greater
than in that of the mother and mistress of a household.
Further, far further, I would not be thought insensible
to the value of culture, not as use in any, even the
highest form, but as beauty and delight, and in that
quality as the adornment of human life and one of the

* This distinction has been ably insisted on by C. H. Payne, D.D.,
LL.D., President of the Ohio Wesleyan University, in an article con-
tributed to the Educational Exhibits Department of the Centennial
Exposition at New Orleans.

rarest factors in human happiness. But on this aspect
it is not needful to comment, or to free it from asper-
sion. It is to be feared that few comparatively of
either sex, of any nation or of any time, will be found
to labour for its acquisition from motives disengaged
from every taint of ambition or eagerness of self-
interest. In the rare case of those who do, there is no
need to fear for the results. In addressing themselves
to their task with the " merry heart " that " goes all
the day " without weariness, " the labour they delight
in physics pain."

When, now some six months ago, I commenced this
inquiry, urged to it by the impression made upon me
by much that had been said concerning the disastrous
effects on female health of the higher education, I was
greatly doubtful of the conclusion to which it would
lead me. Impartial as regards my desires in the
matter, I cannot claim to have been. I was too fully
alive to the growing material needs of the weaker and
more burthened sex to make it a subject of indifference
to me if they should be found hopelessly unequal to
meet the social conditions forced upon them ; but
honestly desiring to learn the truth, and determined
to bear witness to it, however stern and even tragic
that truth might be, I can sincerely say I was, and
have continued to the end. It has been, therefore,
with a gathering sense of reasonable content that, as
I made additions to my knowledge, the conviction

became ever more rooted in my mind, that education which truly answered to the name, was not only innocuous, but positively beneficial to the health of human creatures of either sex. If the facts I have placed before the reader have failed to produce a corresponding impression, I cannot but fear that I have made an imperfect use of, or an unwise selection from, the materials so kindly supplied me.

It does not lie within my present purpose, or my competence, to criticise the methods on which female education is at present pursued, farther than to point out that, the movement being new, it would be contrary to all experience, if there were no mistakes for the future to repair. The wonder is that, all error notwithstanding, so little of damage to health has ever been proved, and so much of benefit has to be set to the positive side of the account.

In admitting the probability of error, I may say that what has most struck me is the general inadequacy of the amount of physical exercise in those high and middle-class schools even, where such exercise is claimed to be a speciality. An hour of calisthenic or light gymnastic movement once a week affords no just balancing up of the body against the mind. Though so large a portion of time could only be allotted to these movements once a week, it seems to me they should be repeated daily in school-hours, and would be found highly beneficial, especially by the younger scholars, in working off the effects of continued attention.   Five minutes of rapid movement between the lessons would restore the circulation of the blood, and brighten and relieve the entire system.

In the colleges where the students are resident, lawn-tennis appears to afford the sole opportunity for that disporting of the muscles so natural and so needful to healthy youth.   Not to cast a word of reflection upon that popular game, a doubt may be allowed of its being all-sufficient in itself as a means of bodily training, and still less as a means of imparting grace and harmony to motion.   Dancing, the art of moving rhythmically to music, as seen in the long-sustained movements of the minuet, would, if systematically studied, go far to remove the reproach of awkwardness, which is not undeserved by English girls.

The ways in which the strain of study is relieved to boys are manifold ; and although in their case it may commonly be carried too far, a leaf out of their book might well be taken in furnishing to girls more varied interests apart from work, and thus lightening the danger of that "worry" over it, which is the chief peril to be guarded against in the feminine composition.

When we come to contemplate that education on a lower plane which in Board schools is supposed to fit the subject for the work of life (an education which necessarily consists more in equipment for the struggle than in simple enrichment of the life), we must, I think, confess that much is at present done which might reasonably be left undone, much omitted which

is of the last importance to those needy ones, in the
fight which lies before them. It is very generally
felt that the vague smattering of theoretic knowledge
which brains, for the most part inert, can acquire in
the short time available, is a mere stone offered in the
place of bread, and that a really serviceable education
for the poorer classes must be more largely technical
or industrial. The retarded intellect is found to learn
to best advantage in *doing;* and through doing it gets
to know and to be.

Not all are gifted with the power to execute even
the commonest work with high efficiency ; but all
may be trained to such a measure of skill in the use
of their hands, as shall make their work not worthless
in the general sum, and a thing to be given in honest
exchange for the means of life.

What is more wanting than all else to the English
man and woman of to-day, elbowed as they are by the
crowds of their own compatriots and the more industrious or more efficient foreigner, is the reinstitution
of the love of labour. It is not to be desired that the
workers should lower their claims. There is no need
that they shall be content with worse housing, worse
clothing, or worse feeding ; let them rather strive even
for better, and also for a fair amount of leisure in which
to recruit and recreate. But work is of the very substance of the life of civilised man, and where that is dis-
organised and half-hearted, disease is at the root of that
life. Only to look upon it in relation to the time it

fills, with most of us it is sheer waste of opportunity to extract from labour no delight. The consciousness of well-doing, if it is but in the right use of a muscle, the pride and joy in skilful accomplishment, is so great an element in human happiness, that all the Palaces of Delight that could rise in response to the dreams of philanthropists, would not compensate for its extinction.

To turn once more from education to life. There is one great want of the woman-worker, without which, though all were skilful and industrious, they would yet remain the victims of cruel oppression. That want, as has been pointed out in an earlier portion of this study, is the want of association on a scale which would embrace all classes of industrial women. Let the dissidents say what they will, the fact is patent to all observers, that men, having combined together and formed unions for themselves, have forced upon employers terms which nothing but combination would have compelled them to concede. To them the wages of labour are often doubled from what they were twenty years ago. They are well fed, well clothed, and not over-worked. But what is the case of the women and girls who belong to them? They are still delivered over, hand and foot, to the mercy of employers, whom the strain of competition impels to cut down expenses to the last farthing, and who take that farthing where best they can get it—from the overwrought efforts, the ignorance and timidity, of unpro-

L

tected women. As we have been truly told by Mr.
Besant : " They are paid starvation wages ; they are
kept in unwholesome rooms ; they are bound to the
longest hours ; they are oppressed with fines. The
girls grow up narrow-chested, stooping, consumptive.
They are used up wholesale." Of such a class, so
uninstructed, so terrified by consequences, and so
unfairly matched in the fight, it is vain to expect
that they shall work deliverance for themselves. Their
freedom from the manifold tyranny of employers,
" sweaters," and go-betweens of all denominations,
must be the gift of the generous hearts and more
capable heads of those who regard the pitiful struggle
from without. It is the most needful, the most pressing bit of work at this moment called for in the world.
We are told that it must be the work of men. Be it
so ; our dearest wish is to see it done. It may well
be that the brutality of employers may be best met
by negotiators carrying something more of material
weight, with a better understanding of commercial
affairs or fallacies, than are often possessed by women.
Such helpers, men, Mr. Besant at their head, are
already in the field, seeking to supplement the efforts,
successful so far as they have gone, of Mr. and Mrs.
Paterson, Mrs. Fawcett, and the little army of large-
hearted men and women who have been the prime
movers in the work, by extending the benefits of association to the sempstresses, slop-workers, and machinists,
the white slaves of our slums and alleys, whom not

so much as the hope of emancipation has at present reached.

Since the earlier portions of this essay were written, the article of Professor Romanes on the leading characters which mentally differentiate men and women, has appeared in the *Nineteenth Century*.

Women have certainly no interest in endeavouring to delude themselves into the belief that their brains are, or could under any circumstances have been, the exact counterpart of those of men; but I am not wholly in accord with the opinion that "no one of those who care most for the women's movement cares one jot to prove that their brains are equal." Let me not here be misunderstood. The equality I would claim is not as things at present stand, not *de facto*, but in original capacity, and even so, an equality in difference, and to some extent of compensation. And this, I think, it is which gives, and will give to such equality more and more, its highest value in the balance of the forces which rule the world.

I am moved to put in this protest because, while it may be regarded by many as sufficient for all practical purpose that the sex shall at length be able to unfold its powers in freedom, and that to this end its legal and social status shall be so redressed as to foster, not impede, its further development, I am persuaded that any view tending to affix a limit to possible progress, is an influence adverse to the best results. In the obscurity in which human destiny is hidden, we are all of us the better for indulging the "larger hope."

In this faith I venture to question some of those conclusions in regard to the female brain, wherein Professor Romanes, in so knightly a fashion, with so many kindly, even flattering admissions, so softly but so surely lets us down.

The fact that the average weight of women's brains is said (I will conclude on adequate proof) to be about five ounces less than that of men, would seem at once, if not for ever, to settle the point in disfavour of equality of intellect, if size and weight were alone adequate to give the full measure of functional efficiency. That such is not the case, that, on the contrary, a small brain with more and deeper convolutions will present a larger surface to stimulating impressions than a larger brain less highly organised, will be acknowledged by no one more readily than by Professor Romanes himself. It is not an unlikely assumption that the facts in regard to the brains of women, have been gathered mostly from the outside, and that a more extended and intimate knowledge of their interior composition might lead to discoveries which would cause the feats occasionally accomplished with so disprized an instrument, to appear less unaccountable. It is certain that things are almost daily being done by women which are compelling their adversaries to a change of front. That some staying power, some inherent force, may be wanted by the smaller and subtler organ, will readily be granted; but the greater pleasure commonly felt by girls in their studies, may be taken as proof that the rapidity of feminine perception tends very materially to lessen labour.

From the showing that in the savage state the disparity of size between the brains of men and women, is less than when both have been subject to civilising influences, the deduction is made by Professor Romanes that woman is by nature less progressive than man. It would be possible, I think, to give another reading to this fact.

In concluding that if woman has not equally progressed, it is that she is not equally progressive, I believe that too little value is assigned to the relatively less intellectually stimulating nature of her work and condition in civilised society, and also to that dead-weight of custom and opinion—the stunting nature of the ideals which have borne upon her. The sole work adapted to develop her full powers in any given direction has been that deriving from the high and onerous charge laid upon her by Nature; the rest may be said chiefly to have consisted of men's "leavings." It is beyond question that such a limitation of opportunity has had good cause to show for itself in a condition of society which is now passing away; but it affords no ground for discouragement if circumstances so little advantageous, should have retarded the development of the woman's mind and will. The construction of the rude hut and the fashioning

and ornamentation of clothes, may not have been so far
in the rear of the cunning needed by the hunter, as the
odds and ends of mental work which women have been
called on to perform in the midst of multiform distrac-
tions, and generally without anything worthy of the
name of teaching. That women should have submitted
to such a state of things may be taken by some as in
itself a proof of inferiority. It is not so. Their sub-
mission is primarily the consequence of the burthen
and labour of maternity ; a burthen which in the mys-
terious course of Nature is being lightened or lifted off
countless numbers of women by no act of their own,
and often to their exceeding regret ; and secondarily,
because owing to the more refined and spiritual character
of the force which the woman can bring to bear upon
circumstances, a state of high social advance is needed
before her characteristic influence can become fully
effective.

If we descend below the savage, and seek among the
higher animals of the order of mammals to which we
belong, the signs of disparity in mental power, we shall
find them even less.

From a sportsman of a type that is now rapidly passing away, one who knew and loved the animals which
contributed to his pleasure, I have heard that the
superior nimbleness and intelligence of the "lady-
pack "—the female hounds, that hunt alternately with
the males—more than compensated the greater pace
and endurance of the dogs. With terriers, spaniels,
retrievers, pointers, it is the same ; wherever the exer-

cise of the faculties has been of a similar nature, the equality of the female has been maintained. Ask the Arab, whose wife, though possibly grey-haired, is a child in knowledge and will, if he has any fault to find with the intelligence of his mare. The female cat is more teachable as well as more attached than the male. But I will not multiply examples. Sufficient has been advanced to justify the belief of those who do " care," that Nature has opposed no insurmountable bar to a progress which we fondly hope to be eternal.

In the meanwhile we may not attempt to refute the proposition of Professor Romanes, that " it is in original work that the disparity " contended for " is most conspicuous." " It is," he tells us, " matter of ordinary comment, that in no one department of creative thought can women be said to have at all approached men, save in fiction." To this one saving clause he does not perhaps accord sufficient importance. For three such names, in our own country alone, as those of Jane Austin, Charlotte Brontë, and George Eliot to appear upon the list in the course of less than fifty years, is no light thing when it is remembered that against them in the same time, from among all the manly host, we can only bring those of Sir Walter Scott, Thackeray, and Dickens as of equal or superior weight. The delicate genius of Jane Austin, nurtured in secret, and self-sustained, contained the living seed of that realism whose fruit, bitter and sweet, has been ripened and over-ripened in our own generation.

Mr. Romanes thinks "the disparity in question, especially suggestive in the case of poetry," seeing the little of special preparation required, and that "at no level of culture has such exercise been ostracised as unfeminine." I cannot but regard this latter assertion as only in a small degree answering to the fact. If the finished product would at no time have reflected unfavourably on the "maker" as a woman, the disposition of mind essential to its achievement on a grand scale, would have met with unmixed condemnation but a few generations ago. Mrs. Browning is, perhaps, the first woman among the moderns, who so dared to dedicate her life. The ideal of character accepted by a dependent creature, slavishly solicitous to please, has always been in direct opposition to that detachment from the small concerns of life and renunciation of its trivial claims, not to speak of duties, which the serious pursuit of art demands. Even now it is tenfold more difficult for a woman than for a man to escape into the silence of her own thoughts; and fifty-fold more hard to get that retreat respected.

Nor are moral causes, the result of dependence, wanting to account for the paucity heretofore of work of high originality on the part of women. The Welsh poetical triad is still perhaps the best definition of genius in few words which has come down to us—

"An eye to see Nature ;
A heart to feel Nature ;
And the boldness that dares follow Nature."

Few will care to deny to women the possession in an even marked degree of the two first of these attributes ; but it is the last which is required to give effect to originality of conception, and that " boldness " is precisely the quality which the teaching of circumstances has in their case tended to suppress.

When we come to compare the sexes, as Professor Romanes has done, in power of judgment, it can hardly be taken to imply innate defect if we find the female deficient in a matter so avowedly dependent on wealth of knowledge and training. As it is, there are questions of deep significance, on which the views of the average woman might, judged from a high standpoint, be held to be in advance of those of the average man. She is less given to " spend her life for that which is not bread, and her labour for that which profiteth not." In other words, the " love " which gives our spiritual measure, is apt in the woman to be higher pitched. When reason is overthrown from emotional causes, the loss or ruin of the home affections is the most potent agent with women : the loss of money with men.

I think we must, many of us, both men and women, have felt some surprise that the claim for superior self-control should have been made for the former. Is it supposed that the chastity which undoubtedly distinguishes women of the better class is so mere a " want-begotten " endowment, that the maintenance of it entitles them to no praise ? Is it believed that beings in whom the sense perceptions are specially

acute, bear pain with silent endurance as liking it?
The tears of the woman are more ready because
she is quicker to feel, and this mode of betraying
emotion is not held particularly to discredit her; but I
think it would be difficult to prove that her temper,
however shown, was commonly less under control than
that of men.   Of hysterics among women I am persuaded that a great deal more is heard than seen, and
that the disease is unknown among those who have
found work fitted to their powers; but the language
is sadly in want of some term which would imply the
same phase of emotional outbreak in the other sex.
In view of the derivation of the word "hysteria," the
proprieties of speech forbid us to call the utter loss of
mental balance which is seen in the half-childish, half-
animal rage of men, often provoked by the merest
trifles, by that name; but such exhibitions are very
certainly the brutal analogue of the more purely nervous
affection, and are of much more frequent occurrence.

In regard to the power possessed by the female
sex of bearing the physical strain demanded by a
liberal education, the testimony of Professor Romanes
goes beyond, even far beyond, any that I have set
before the reader in the course of this essay, or any, it
must be said, that I could feel able to endorse.   It is
inconceivable by me that a growing girl, however good
the "stuff" of which she was made, could sustain
without damage labours such as the young correspondent of Professor Romanes claims as the day's

work of herself and her schoolmates. But it must also be said that at no school with which the course of my inquiries has brought me acquainted, would such infringement of the rules have been endured.

Eighteen hours a day, of study! Why not twenty? —why not twenty-four? If we are to accept the statement, we can only imagine that the parents of these young girls, desiring to disgrace the cause of female culture, have offered their daughters as victims of intemperate application to study, as the Romans made their Helots drunk for the warning of their sons.

It is in the time employed in preparation at home that the evil of over-strain is most to be feared. It is the duty laid in the printed rules, which are issued in nearly all day-schools, upon the mother, to see and report to the mistresses if the amount of work given is more than can be accomplished in the appointed time. The "abuse," which Professor Romanes justly characterises as "insane," thus recoils upon the parents or guardians of the young girls so left to their uncontrolled and self-defeating ambitions.

The remarks I have hazarded on the circumstances conditioning the development of the two sexes, are the expression of no vain desire to claim for women a present equality with men in force of intellect, or, in some respects, of character; their object is to vindicate, as at least an open question, the inherent capacity of the retarded sex for illimitable progress upon its own lines.

In carrying our speculations back with the physiologist to the lowest beginnings of life in which sex is
apparent, it would appear that active strength is generally, if not universally, the characteristic of the male,
swiftness and subtlety that of female intelligence; and
this impress we may expect, that each will bear to
the end.   What I think may fairly be maintained is,
that the widely separate set of circumstances which
have attended their unfoldings has tended to exagge-
rate their original dispositions; and this scarcely more
to the disadvantage of the feminine than the masculine brain.

We must all admit that the work of the world is
often very imperfectly accomplished, and that it shows
signs of being hacked at with a rather blunt instrument.   If the one sex is frequently feeble, the other
is almost universally slow, and its want of fineness of
perception is such, that entire sympathy between a
man and woman is one of the rarest perfections to be
found in life.   The most devoted of wives scarcely
looks for it in the tenderest of husbands.   This want
it is, this slowness and bluntness, and not intentional
obduracy, which has left the non-militant sex for
countless generations after the primitive stage, in
which it seemed right and natural, in a legal condition of anomalous helplessness and oppression.   In no
part of the Western world has the law been less protective to women than in England, where its amelio-
rations are of recent date, and have been yielded in

response to the efforts of women themselves. But for the sound and generous instincts of the majority of Englishmen, this island, whereof the sons have been among the first to appreciate the good gifts of freedom, would have been a very house of bondage and its attendant evils to its daughters.

But while recognising to the full the general kindliness of disposition which has formed a counterweight to bad laws, and even taking into account a certain stimulation of the protective instinct in men, due to a sense of the disabilities under which women have suffered, it must never be forgotten that long after the time in which male protection had for millions of women become impossible, disqualifications which made their struggle for themselves the harder, remained wholly unheeded by those who had the making and the mending of the laws. Let what may be affirmed to the contrary, it is women who have wrought out, and are still working at, their own deliverance. It would be impossible to maintain that the Married Women's Property Act, and other reforms, would have been carried in our time but for the Suffrage League. No one of the changes in the law regarding women, which do tardy credit to our legislature, dates farther back than its establishment. It would be invidious to mention but a few of the best-known names of those women who have been working to this end for more than thirty years. Their bearers have laboured through the toil and heat of the day; they have braved ridicule, and even disgust. They have done their public-spirited work as best they were able, and posterity will hold them in honour.

But little of what is still due has been achieved in regard to the most criminal of legal abuses—the law which can award more than the pound of flesh to be taken from the place nearest the heart of a virtuous mother, which cruel Shylocks, standing by the letter of the enactment, have been found to claim. Those who heard or read the debate on the so-called "Infants' Bill" of March 1884, are not likely to forget the incapacity of most of the men who took part in it, for so much as a perception of natural justice as between themselves and their legal subordinates. It is well that there are Portias among us still, women who, as "Daniels," can at least make out a case for judgment.

In concluding this imperfect review, this mere glance over the wide field of the new relation of women to work, I feel that, with the exception of the authoritative opinions to which I have been privileged to give publicity, there is little that is likely to interest the expert in the foregoing pages. It is to the large number of persons standing outside the question at issue, but willing to take a more intelligent interest in it, that they are chiefly addressed. For such, the nature of the common objections to the higher education and employment of women will have been made clear; and it is hoped that whatever of

weight certain of those objections may still retain for
many minds, it will be evident to all that the movement of advance is no temporary fashion or arbitrary
decree, but the outcome of a force as inevitable as fate
itself.   Women in large numbers are called to the
fight; they have been engaged in it more or less for
many generations, and have been worsted in helpless
thousands.   They feel at last the necessity of equipping
themselves for the conflict, and are arming.   What
more is to be said ?

Something, I think, if our whole feeling in relation
to the new order is to be expressed.   A fight; it is
a word of dread.   It is hard for faith itself to overcome
all fear of what it may give as well as of what it may
take away.   The combative qualities are not amiable
in themselves.   May we hope that the strength of
womanhood will adopt of them but what is needful to
give firmness and decision to effort, and will temper
the remainder and infuse it with its own essence ?

So far from any advantage accruing, either to
themselves or to society, from women becoming
less women, they would be better, as I think, for
becoming more.   All under this head that is to be
desired is the raising of the existing ideal.   This
done, it would be well that women should carry their
womanhood intact into any work to which they
can substantiate their calling.   Theory, as we have
seen, has broken down with regard to them in the
physical sphere, the natural infirmity with which they

have been charged being merely the result of circumstances; and there is abundant reason to believe that it is not wholly in defect that the female brain, even as at present conditioned, differs from the male. It can scarcely be doubtful that it is in striking out its own course that it will achieve the best results. In any case, we are justified in holding that, from the freer conditions of life and labour in the future, no new genus will be evolved—no sexless creature—but that womanhood will remain one and the same as before; not sharply defined, as Dr. Richardson expects, into two classes—the bearers of children, or what have been called the "brood-mothers," on the one hand, and the workers with brain or body, on the other. Human nature being what it is, a "caste" distinct as that here contemplated will never obtain a place in the system of things. The woman of trained faculty will be continually going over to the supposed enemy, and swelling the ranks of wife and motherhood; all the more readily, in certain cases, in that she is capable of adding something to the marital exchequer. On the whole, we may be permitted to hope that Nature will continue to hold in charge her final work. Custom, if potent, is not omnipotent. It has not made woman by its arbitrary decrees, and the withdrawal of those decrees will not unmake her.

I have no words wherewith to express the depth of my conviction that it is a thing above all things to be desired that the sex should hold fast the virtues learnt in a long past of repression, which, while never just, has been often protective, and always, and through all, most kindly in result. No merely intellectual gain could compensate the loss of the humblest of the virtues acquired in the course of this prolonged discipline. It is matter for comfortable reflection, that whatever amenities of outward circumstance may accrue to the woman's life in the future, the wholesome severities of Nature can never be wholly withdrawn. It would be better that the weight which has retarded her progress should continue to the last to limit her powers of production in the mental sphere, than that she should lose the impulse to sacrifice, born of the tenderness which her work in Nature has primarily developed, and wherewith through her it has gifted the race.

Maternal affection is too merely instinctive to be rightly reckoned a virtue in itself; but it supplies the nidus of a love related to that which moves the world, and is the fulfilling of all law.

It is possible that the impulse to personal sacrifice, causing the subject to lay aside its own claims to demands from without, may lay a heavy tax upon women's powers to the end; but it is also conceivable that the sacrificial emotions, when not called upon for an expression too sustained and absolute, will be found helpful rather than the reverse, even to art itself. History is not wanting in examples of men who, having made Molochs of their genius, have been pre-

M

sumably losers rather than gainers by the immolation
of their manhood to an idol. I cling to the belief
that "no man's work is greater than his soul." And a
soul incapable of the madness of generous sacrifice is
incapable of rising to the height of the noblest achievement. "The resolution of the less into the greater is
the true wisdom of life." Let us hold by the highest
good of which we can obtain a purchase in following
out that path of destiny towards which necessity is so
ruthlessly driving us. Those mostly who have not
lost faith in a shaping and guiding Power, above all
law which is known to man, will be inclined to trust
in all things the salutary operation of its seemingly
inflexible will.

There is a disposition abroad to attribute the lack
of gentleness, with the restlessness and love of excitement very observable in the manners of the day, in
the case of women, in whom it is most to be depre-
cated, to the wider horizons which have lately been
opened to them. There might seem to be some colour
for this accusation, were it not that the lack of gentleness more especially, is most observable precisely in
that class which stands most aloof from the movement for advanced culture. High fashion does not
imply high birth, any more than high birth implies
high breeding, but fashion gives the tone to the manners of a generation, nevertheless. It is from this
narrow world that loudness and self-assertion now
percolate downwards. Here are to be seen in perfec-

tion those attitudes of mind and body which, while intending to proclaim the utmost ease of disregard for others, do most truly betray the lurking disesteem of self. For self-respect, if not the parent, is at least the nurse of reverence. The manners of " society " are aggressive because society is too vast. It is a well-dressed mob, that hustles and jostles, knowing that a good place is to be got by pushing. In the restlessness which is also so marked a feature of our time—the feeling that no one is where he would be, but is hurrying to get there—other influences than that above noted are at work, chief among which is the spirit, not of sad and earnest, but of heedless agnosticism, with the loosening of all bonds, human and divine, which accompanies it. As Miss Clough has so clearly pointed out in the letter quoted in an earlier page, the tendency of a life really studious is the reverse of all this. An undue occupation with the things of the mind may be more justly charged with favouring timidity in social intercourse, as in action generally, than with adding to evils with which it has in fact no affinity.

Finally, who shall say there is nothing to deplore when the old order changes ? There may be developments of character, sweet and noble developments, for which the opportunities will be less abundant in the future. The gentle self-effacement and tender dependence of the women of bygone generations was not without its charm. But of what avail are regrets,

which can alter nothing? The extended activity of
women is an accomplished fact; its results are on
their trial. We have arrived, consciously or otherwise, at one of those determining moments in the
history of the race when a new departure in progress
is inaugurated. If the path upon which women have
entered be the true path of their destiny, they will
follow it to the end, and will probably work out upon
that broad highway a result more beneficial to humanity generally than any that could have been arrived
at on a side issue.

APPENDIX.

Miss Margaret Mackillip, one of the Principals of the Ladies' Collegiate School, Londonderry, sends notes concerning health of distinguished students of this school, accompanied by the following remarks, viz. : "The dates I have given represent the time I have known the students, and as they have nearly all been resident pupils, I speak with accurate knowledge of their health. I have only noted our most distinguished workers, sixteen in number. My unqualified testimony is, *that if there is proper care of the health, the intellectual quickening is of great benefit to the physical condition of girls.*"

LIST OF THE PUPILS.

Charlotte Young. 1879–85. Girton Scholar. Natural Science Tripos, second class and various honors. — Perfectly robust health. No illness of any serious nature and no weakness of constitution. Cheery, practical, and energetic.

Anna G. Hogben. 1879–86. Girton Scholar. Gained a place in the Classical Tripos List, Cambridge 1886, and various honours. — Perfectly good health, though not very robust in physique. Some slight illness at Girton through overwork. A student who worked without due regard to health.

Maggie M'Vicker. 1880–87. Intermediate Student. Various honours. — Clever, fair student; splendid and constant good health. Has the advantage of a fine physique.

Louisa Young. 1880–87. Intermediate. Now teaching in India. Junior Grade Gold Medal for Mathematics, and various honours. — Clever student. Fine physique and constant good health.

Bessie Anderson. 1881–83. Senior Grade Gold Medal for Mathematics. — Clever student. Not very robust, though no serious illness—Nervous or rather anxious temperament.

Amelia Hurst. 1880–87. Intermediate and Royal University, various honours. — Clever student, but not *too* industrious. Magnificent health ; never a day's illness.

Elizabeth Wray. 1880–86. Intermediate. £20 (tenable for three years). — Anxious student. Weak physique. No illness, but required care to keep up the health.

Sophia Young. 1880–87. Intermediate. Royal University. £20 (tenable for three years), and other honours. — Industrious student. Good general health ; vigorous ; energetic.

EMILY BUCHANAN. 1881–87. Intermediate. Now teaching in England. £20 (tenable for three years).

Good student. Perfect health ; no illness of any kind.

MARY KENNEDY. 1882–87. Intermediate and Girton. Senior Grade Medal for Mathematics, and other honours.

Clever, close student. Rude health ; never a day's illness.

FLORA FULLERTON. 1883–87. Intermediate. A gold medal in English, and one for first place in grade, and various other honours.

Very distinguished student. Magnificent health ; not a day's illness. Cheerful, vigorous, energetic.

LIZZIE DICK. 1884–87. Intermediate. Gold Medal in Mathematics, and other honours.

Very good student. Very young ; not particularly robust, but constant good health and good spirits.

MARY ATKINSON. 1885–87. Royal University. Honours in English and French, and Draper's Scholarship, value in all £105.

Very good student. Eyes suffered from study, but general health good.

MARY LITTLE. 1885–86. £25 (for two years).

Extremely clever student. Very delicate constitution, and certainly failed in health through trying to compass too much.

MAUDE YOUNG. From a child. Intermediate. £15 (for three years).

Steady student ; broke down for a few months, and had to leave school at a critical time.

EMILY STEWART. 1884–87. Intermediate. £15 (for three years).

Good student, and perfect health always.

Extracts from a Special Committee of the Association of Collegiate Alumæ in the United States (ANNIE G. HOWES, Chairman), together with Statistical Tables collected by the Massachusetts Bureau of Statistics of Labour.

After the completion of the college course, we find the graduates occupied in various ways. Of those who have entered upon household duties, 24 did housework only, and 270 in connection with some other occupation ; 37 were engaged in professional work only, and 112 in professional and other occupation ; 130 took up teaching as their sole occupation, while 224 were engaged in teaching in conjunction with other occupations. In the same way it is seen that 249 were occupied with work of an intellectual nature, 107 with study, 105 philanthropy, and 210 with social duties, all of which occupations were usually carried forward in connection with other occupation or attention to other cares and duties.

Of the 705 graduates, 509, or 72.2 per cent., are single at the present time, and 196, or 27.8 per cent., are married. These 196 have been married, on the average, 6.7 years ; 130 have had children, and 66 have had no children. Of the whole number of children, or 263, 232 are living, and 31 have died ; of the children living, 208 are in good health, 15 in poor, and for 9 the health is not given. The average present age of children living is 6.0 years.

Of the whole number of graduates from or concerning whom returns were received, but 8 were reported as being dead.

The physical condition of each graduate has been shown to be either "excellent," "good," "fair," "indifferent," or "poor" for the following five-age periods : from 3 to 8 years of age ; from 8 to 14 years of age ; at time of entering college, during college life, and since graduation. In the summary table, which we now present, we shall show the number and percentage, for each of the five-age-periods named, of those whose health has been excellent or good, the number and percentage of those whose health has been fair, and the number and percentage of those whose health has been indifferent or poor. In the analysis of the comparison tables, so far as health is concerned, this condensation of the state of health will be used, as best representing the extremes, or good and poor health, and the intermediate state, or fair health. The summary table of physical condition for all colleges only follows : —

| | PHYSICAL CONDITION. | | | | | | SUMMARY. | | | |
| AGE PERIODS. | EXCELLENT OR GOOD. | | FAIR. | | INDIFFERENT OR POOR. | | AGGREGATES. | |
	Number.	Per cent.	Number.	Per cent.	Number.	Per cent.	Number.	Per cent.
From 3 to 8 years of age, . .	541	76.74	13	1.84	151	21.42		
From 8 to 14 years of age, . .	517	73.33	21	2.98	167	23.69	705	100.00
At entering college	551	78.16	14	1.98	140	19.86		
During college life	528	74.89	55	7.80	122	17.31		
Since graduation,	549	77.87	36	5.11	120	17.02		

From the foregoing summary of physical condition, it will be seen that the results for the specified state of health, for each of the periods considered, vary but slightly. For instance, for those who have been in excellent or good health, we find 541, or 76.74 per cent. of the whole number were in excellent health between the ages of three and eight years ; 517 or 73.33 per cent. between eight and fourteen years of age ; 551 or 78.16 per cent. at entering college ; 528 or 74.87 per cent. during college life ; and 549, or 77.87 per cent., since graduation. If we consider these percentages as indicating for certain of the periods a falling off from the standard of excellent or good, and also subsequent recovery wholly or in part, we find that 3.41 per cent. less report their state of health to be unchanged in the second period as compared with the first. This loss of health was more than recovered in the next period, or during college life. In the fourth period another decline is noted, 3.27 per cent. less reported excellent or good health. This decline was practically overcome in the fifth period, or since graduation, by an increase in excellent or good health of 2.98 per cent. The general average percentage showing excellent or good health for all periods is 76.20 per cent. In the same way the fluctuation in the percentages showing fair health and indifferent or poor health can be easily traced. For the period marking health during college life, it will be seen that the decline of 3.27 per cent. from excellent or good health is comprehended in the increase of number reporting fair health for the same period. The percentage of increase for fair health for this period as compared with that preceding is 5.82 per cent., the excess of this percentage of increase over the percentage of loss reported for excellent or good health being accounted for by an increase of health during college life among those who at the time of entering college were in indifferent or poor health. In other words, during college life 3.27 per cent. declined from excellent or good to fair, and 2.55 per cent. advanced from indifferent or poor to fair health. It should be noticed, also, that although 21.42 per cent. and 23.69 per cent. respectively were in indifferent or poor health for the first two periods named, but 17.31 per cent. and 17.02 per cent. respectively reported a similar state of health during college life, and since graduation showing a steady advance so far as indifferent or poor health is concerned. From the table showing nervousness it appears that 28 were naturally nervous before entering college, 74 are nervous at the present time, 231 were naturally nervous before entering college, and are also nervous at the present time, that is, have always been nervous, while 372 are not naturally of a nervous disposition.

SUMMARY OF RESULTS.

Referring briefly to the results as shown by the tables, it appears :—

That the graduates are largely of American parentage ; that the greater part of them spent their childhood in the country, and had a fair amount of outdoor exercise daily.

That 57 per cent. began study in a school, and 41 per cent. at home, the remaining 2 per cent. failing to answer ; that the average age at which they began study was 5.64 years, at entering college 18.35 years, at graduating from college 22.39 years ; and that the average present age is 28.58 years.

That during college life the majority studied but moderately ; that 44 per cent. did not worry over their studies or affairs ; that they were generally regular as regards hours for eating and sleeping, took a proper amount of physical exercise daily ; that, as a rule, they entered society but little, and for the most part had college room-mates.

That since graduation all seem to have found congenial occupation, a great many as teachers, while eight only are occupied with social duties to the exclusion of other occupation.

That about one-fourth have married, and that of the whole number of children borne by them, the greater part are living and in good health.

That, for all the various periods of their lives, the health of over three-fourths of the graduates has been either excellent or good ; that during college life a slight falling off from excellent or good health is apparent, resulting in an increase in number reporting fair health, while, on the other hand, the number reporting indifferent or poor health is smaller than for any preceding period, and but slightly in access of the number reporting the same conditions of health for the succeeding period, or since graduation.

That over one-half of the graduates are not and have not been troubled with nervousness, and that nearly 25 per cent. have had no trouble at any time during the menstrual period.

That about 60 per cent. have had some disorder ; the more common disorders reported relating to the stomach, liver, bowels, lungs, nervous system, generative organs, neuralgic and rheumatic affections, and to a certain extent to the heart and brain.

That the most prevalent cause of disorders is constitutional weakness, the other causes being bad sanitary conditions, intellectual overwork, emotional strain, and physical accident.

That the various conditions of childhood, as shown in the comparison tables, have had no marked influence for good or evil upon the present health of graduates.

That the present health of graduates seems to have been affected according as their parents have enjoyed either good or poor health, the figures showing 3 per cent. increase in health for those whose parents were both in good health, and a decline in health of over 17 per cent. for those whose parents were both in poor health.

That so far as inherited tendency to disease is considered, a decline in health has also taken place, as compared with the average good health of all the graduates, those inheriting tendency to disease from either parent showing a decline in health of 3 to 5 per cent., those inheriting tendency to disease from both parents of nearly 20 per cent., while in the case of those who have no hereditary tendency to disease, there has been an increase of nearly 3 per cent. in good health.

That during college life about 20 per cent. show a deterioration in health, 60 per cent. no change, and 20 per cent. an improvement ; that for those who enter college at sixteen years of age or under, an increased deterioration in health of between 10 and 11 per cent. as compared with those who entered at a later age is observed, and of over 8 per cent. as compared with the whole number whose health deteriorated.

That during college life there was nearly 2½ per cent. less deterioration in health as compared with the deterioration in health reported during working time by the working girls of Boston.

The facts which we have presented would seem to warrant the assertion, as the legitimate conclusion to be drawn from a careful study of the tables, that the seeking of a college education on the part of women does not in itself necessarily entail a loss of health or serious impairment of the vital forces. Indeed, the tables show this so conclusively, that there is little need, were it within our province, for extended discussion of the subject.

The graduates, as a body, entered college in good health, passed through the course of study prescribed without material change in health, and since graduation, by reason of the effort required to gain a higher education, do not seem to have become unfitted to meet the responsibilities or bear their proportionate share of the burdens of life.

It is true that there has been, and it was to be expected that there would be, a certain deterioration in health on the part of some of the graduates. On the other hand, an almost identical improvement in health for a like number was reported, showing very plainly that we must look elsewhere for the causes of the greater part of this decline in health during college life. If we attempt to trace the cause, we find that this deterioration is largely due, not to the requirements of college life particularly, but to predisposing causes natural to the graduates themselves, born in them, as it were, and for which college life or study should not be made responsible. A girl constitutionally weak is always at a disadvantage, and naturally would suffer a deterioration in health, temporary possibly or even permanent, if at the most trying period of her life, from eighteen to twenty-two years, she seeks superior education. At the same time, we should not fail to emphasise the fact that fully 30 per cent. of the total deterioration in health during college life was from excellent to good only. In the case of those graduates who studied severely, even, the facts reported concerning their physical condition do not show that they have suffered materially from the effects of close application, but that they have since graduation returned to the normal condition reported by them at the time of entering college.

In conclusion, it is sufficient to say that the female graduates of our colleges and universities do not seem to show, as the result of their college studies and duties, any marked difference in general health from the average health likely to be reported by an equal number of women engaged in other kinds of work, or, in fact, of women generally without regard to occupation followed.

PRINTED BY BALLANTYNE, HANSON AND CO.
EDINBURGH AND LONDON

For EU product safety concerns, contact us at Calle de José Abascal, 56–1°, 28003 Madrid, Spain or eugpsr@cambridge.org.

www.ingramcontent.com/pod-product-compliance
Ingram Content Group UK Ltd.
Pitfield, Milton Keynes, MK11 3LW, UK
UKHW012344130625
459647UK00009B/517